Inspirations for Creating Sparkling Attitudes

HEART
of a MOTHER

Compiled by

Sheryl L. Roush

Creative Communications
San Diego, California

A Sparkle-Tudes!® Series Book
Published by Creative Communications
A division of Sparkle Presentations
Post Office Box 2373, La Mesa, California 91943 USA

If brought to the attention of the author/publisher, verified credit for quotations
will be attributed in the next printing (or next update).
Biblical quotes, cultural proverbs and sayings are used
randomly from various translations.
Send contributions to Sheryl@SparklePresentations.com

Visit our website at:
www.SparklePresentations.com

Second Printing June 2006

Library of Congress Cataloging-in-Publication Data
Roush, Sheryl Lynn.
Sparkle-Tudes: Heart of a Mother
Inspirations for Creating Sparkling Attitudes/Sheryl L. Roush
Includes index.
ISBN 978-1-880878-11-9

1. Self-Help   2. Inspirational   3. Women's Issues

2006905277

Front cover painting by Suzan Tusson-McNeil.
Sparkling Heart design by Cath Kachur.
Book design and compilation by Sheryl Roush.
Cover design by Drew Design.
Interior design and production by Sheryl Roush and Drew Design.

Printed in the United States of America.

A Mother's Love

A Mother's heart lights up the whole world
So full of love, commitment and passion
There is never a quota or any ration.

The heart of a Mother is bold and strong
Holding a space for the family's evolution
For love and peace is the only solution.

Born to be compassionate, devoted and strong
Her heart always beating to the vibration of love
A Mother receives energy sent from above.

Always beaming with divine inspiration
Mothers unite, holding hands together
Creating a circle of love - forever.

A Mother's love creates a fine lineage of care
Love layered upon infinite love
Hand fitted within the family glove.

A Mother loves with her whole heart
Breathing in and out a love so intense
Her whole world becomes immense.

We feel, we teach, we expand and we soar
Flying amid the possibilities of life
We may be single mother, grandmother or wife.

Jodi Seidler is a The Mother of Re-Invention, single parent expert and the
creator of www.makinglemonade.com, The Single Parent Network

✳ 3 ✳

About the Cover

ARTIST BIOGRAPHY: Suzan Tusson-McNeil

As a little girl I loved to paint alongside my Dad with my own canvas and bright acrylic colors. However, a personal tragedy occurred in my youth and I stopped painting. A few years ago an artist suggested we trade private art lessons for personal coaching. I felt an electric rush and agreed. As my quivering hand swashed acrylic paint onto the canvas, long held tears streamed down. My body and palette dropped in unison to the floor. My reclaimed artist grieved her lost time and expression. With self-forgiveness, I have loved my little artist back to life.

I now paint as a passionate pastime adorning the walls of our home with my colorful expressions. My sister, Adele, and our Mother, who has passed on, inspired the art piece for the cover, *Heart of a Mother.* I also give tribute to the Great Creator who guided my hands during this process.

Adele shared that 'being a Mother was like having her heart walking outside in front of her.' My Mother was the continual cheerleader along my life's sidelines. When painting, I feel her warm gaze, and it helps to channel my emotions onto the canvas. I created heart shaped bodies for the children, with their heart strings firmly attach-ed to their Mother. The Heart of a Mother is grounded in the core of Mother Earth. I celebrate Mothers and their endless reservoirs of love.

Finally, I honor creativity. May you express your heart in whatever way calls. Listen.

www.wisdomquestcoaching.com

Mothers

Somebody said it takes about six weeks to get back to normal
after you've had a baby...
Somebody doesn't know that once you're a mother,
"Normal," is history.
Somebody said you learn how to be a mother by instinct...
Somebody never took a three-year-old shopping.
Somebody said being a mother is boring...
Somebody never rode in a car driven by a teenager
with a driver's permit.
Somebody said if you're a "good" mother,
your child will "turn out good..."
Somebody thinks a child comes with directions and a guarantee.
Somebody said "good" mothers never raise their voices...
Somebody never came out the back door just in time to see her child
hit a golf ball through the neighbor's kitchen window.
Somebody said you don't need an education to be a mother...
Somebody never helped a fourth grader with her math.
Somebody said you can't love the fifth child
as much as you love the first...
Somebody doesn't have five children.
Somebody said a mother can find all the answers
to her child-rearing questions in the books...
Somebody never had a child stuff beans up his nose or in his ears.
Somebody said the hardest part of being a mother
is labor and delivery...
Somebody never watched her "baby" get on the bus for the first day
of kindergarten, or on a plane headed for military "boot camp."
Somebody said a mother can do her job with her eyes closed
and one hand tied behind her back...
Somebody never organized four giggling Brownies to sell cookies.
Somebody said a mother can stop worrying
after her child gets married...
Somebody doesn't know that marriage
adds a new son-or daughter-in-law to a mother's heartstrings.
Somebody said a mother's job is done
when her last child leaves home...
Somebody never had grandchildren.
Somebody said your mother knows you love her,
so you don't need to tell her...
Somebody isn't a mother.

— Author Unknown—

From My Heart to Yours

This book is dedicated to Mothers everywhere!
The most important, most complicated, and most endearing of all relationships we have with another is the relationship we have with our Mother. You have given us birth, held us, and released us – to continue to grow on our own. Your love is unconditional, forgiving, forbearing, expanding. Having a child is like having your heart walking around outside of your body... attached by Heartstrings.

You have given us gifts of your wisdom, fortitude, perseverance, intuition, faith, humanity, humor, compassion, mercy and grace–life itself–and the greatest of these, your love! You have taught us to love ourselves, love others, believe in our dreams, and take time to enjoy the journey to our own motherhood. We thank you–and we celebrate YOU! The poems, stories and tributes within these pages are dedicated to you.

Many of the women contributing submissions shared that this was the most challenging journaling they had ever done. Many tears were shed in the process; with much healing, thoughtfulness and gratitude. Abundant appreciation to each of the contributors! Thank you for sharing YOUR tributes, your memories, your heartfelt words!

Special thanks and acknowledgements to dear friends and colleagues Lisa R. Delman, author of *Dear Mom*, for helping women express their feelings to their mothers with the *Letters from the Heart Project,* and Mary Marcdante, author of *My Mother, My Friend,* empowering communication NOW with your mother. Both are doing amazing work in the area of healing mother-daughter relationships.

Thanks to Suzan Tusson-McNeil who custom painted the heartstrings mother-and-children cover for this publication.

Loving thanks and gratitude to my own parent, Hiram and Beverly Roush, for helping me become all of who I am today! Thank you for showing me love, and in all the trying times I needed it the most!

From My Heart to Yours,
Sheryl

Table of Contents

Table of Contents

Table of Contents

Table of Contents

HEART
of a MOTHER

Heart of A Mother

10 Ways to Open Your Heart to Your Mother

Dear Mom, I've Always Wanted You to Know...Letters from the Heart

1. Honor Yourself

Take a few moments to honor and appreciate yourself. Acknowledge your courage to open your heart, articulate your emotions on paper, and grow from your willingness to write a letter to your mother. When you take the time to reflect inwardly, you nurture yourself.

2. Reconnect to Your Heart

Take some deep breaths and connect emotionally with your mother. Self-reflection requires a change of pace of what you may be accustomed to. Allow yourself the time to relax. Create a quiet, private space to write your letter. Perhaps choose a favorite place in nature, listen to soothing music such as Enya, Steve Halpern, or classical music, or enjoy your favorite food or tea in a place where you feel peaceful.

3. Create a Desired Outcome

Expand your thoughts beyond your present image of your mother and your relationship. If you are encountering challenges with your relationship, be open to experiencing her in a new light. For example, you may want to resolve past hurts or be more loving toward her. You may want to understand more or develop more of an appreciation for her. This exercise is not about dumping on your mother. It is about exploring your emotions through letter writing, resolving past hurts, and experiencing positive shifts within yourself and your relationship with your mother. Aiming for a desired outcome will guide you to be more centered on what is most important. Let the process unfold naturally. Dianne Collins, creator-author of *Quantum Think®*, says, "It is like planting the seeds for a garden of love and appreciation, honor, and respect. In such a relationship garden, even if weeds sprout, you can just handle them and remain in awe of the beauty blossoming there."

Write, visualize, and feel one positive expression from writing the letter.

4. Express Your Feelings Honestly

Eliose Ristad says, "Feel all the opposites that comprise your being human. Feel the power in these opposing forces within you. Without these opposites, you would be as bland and characterless as unsalted mush."

Certain words listed below may prompt a particular feeling you have or have had toward your mother. To release a negative feeling, you might want to write about that feeling and see what you discovered about yourself in the process. This exercise is about acknowledging a specific feeling, releasing it, and learning from it. It is about letting go of what holds you back. If it evokes a positive feeling, you may discover something new about your mother. Remember, this is a springboard to guide you. Only you know what is true in your heart.

Choose one or two emotions listed below when you think of your mother and write about them. Also describe what you learned about yourself through this process.
- Fear
- Embarrassment
- Joy, Celebration, Enthusiasm
- Sorrow, Sadness, Regret, Remorse, Grief, Guilt
- Freedom, Letting Go, Joy, Release
- Gratitude, Appreciation, Respect
- Courage, Bravery, Risk Taking
- Control, Regret, Bossiness, Criticism
- Epiphany, Forgiveness, Insight
- Resentment, Anger, Betrayal, Jealousy, Competition, Estrangement
- Love, Understanding, Acceptance, Compassion, Forgiveness, Peace of Mind

5. Appreciate All of the Memories

Be grateful for all of the memories you have with your mother and learn from them. Recall defining moments, challenging times, or particular gestures. You may not know how you feel until you put pen to paper. Simply let your ideas unfold naturally without forcing them. Welcome your uncensored emotions without judgments. If judgments arise, gently release them as part of the process. Be patient and loving to yourself.

As you revisit your feelings, jot down 5 memories of your mother. You may have fewer than 5 memories or you may have more, but 5 is a place to begin.

6. Explore Different Perspectives

We view our relationships according to our perspective on life. Many times, we cannot see beyond our own experiences. As you think of your relationship with your mother, begin viewing her in various roles in her life: as a woman, wife, daughter, grandmother, volunteer, professional, and friend. Seeing your mother in a new light can provide a fresh perspective on the way you view her, yourself, and your relationship.

Write down 5 or more things you've noticed about yourself and your mother when you explore these different roles.

7. Think From Generation to Generation

As daughters, we may primarily focus on the relationship with only our mothers. We blame our mothers for the beliefs they may have adopted from their mothers, and so on. If we explore the past, we notice that certain behaviors have been passed on to us from generation to generation.

Jot down 5 of these belief systems. If you are not sure about those in other generations, speculate and write them down anyway.

8. Go Beyond Stereotypical Expectations

We often expect our mothers to be a certain way from the cultural messages we grew up with, and when they do not meet our image, we feel disappointed and even resentful. Often, our expectations cloud us from appreciating our mothers for who they are. Once we can identify with our false expectations, we can honor their uniqueness.

Jot down 5 expectations you have now or once had with your mother. Also write down what you discovered from this process.

9. Make Challenges Your Greatest Gifts

We often blame our mothers for all the hardships we experienced while growing up and the hardships we still experience: for not being there; for being there in the "wrong way," for the woman we are; for the woman we are not; for all the challenges we had to overcome because of our mothers. Many times, our challenges turn into resentments, which prevent us from being in the present moment. Any feelings of anger may have begun with our mother, may even quickly move into our other relationships.

Write down 5 resentments you have about your mother.
Explore your challenges with your mother as gifts and write down what you discovered.

10. Open Your Heart

The objective of these 10 exercises is to examine your relationship with your mother from new perspectives and open your heart. When we view our experiences in new ways, we enrich our relations with others and ourselves. Feel free to use some or all of these exercises to support you in writing your letter.

Begin your letter now. Be true to your personal voice. It will always lead you to the right place. The rest will follow.

10 QUESTIONS TO PONDER

1. What did you learn about yourself from your experiences with your mother?
2. What did your mother represent to you growing up?
3. What did you want but did not get from your mother?
4. If you only had one day to resolve the issues with your mother, what would you say?
5. What do you constantly complain about regarding your mother?
6. What kind of relationship would you like to have with your mother?
7. Is there one event with your mother that changed the course of your life?
8. What resentments or dislikes do you have regarding your mother?
9. What do you admire about your mother?
10. What does your mother represent to you now?

—Lisa R. Delman, Speaker, Author of *Dear Mom, I've Always Wanted You to Know... Daughters Share Letters from the Heart*, Penguin 2005. Founder and visionary of the international Heart Project. Encourages women to articulate their emotions sacredly on paper initiating a journey that often leads to self-discovery, healing past wounds, and an opportunity to feel liberated. www.TheHeartProject.com

Adopted with Love

Adopted Daughters and Their Circle of Love

If I ever felt an expression of love from my daughters, this was one beautiful experience that will forever stay with me... Last Tuesday, my birthday, my daughters asked me to take them to an activity in the evening. When I arrived to pick them up, they emerged from the house carrying a cake adorned with at least a dozen lighted candles. Their faces were aglow from the candlelight, left an indelible imprint on my mind, as they sang "Happy Birthday." In their scurry to get the cake ready on time, the cool icing caused the freshly baked cake still warm out of the oven to fall apart on one side. For me this birthday cake was made with so much love, I never would have noticed. It was perfect. A memory to savour forever. To top it off, they secretly planned a little surprise party at my favorite pizza restaurant! My daughter Lauren visited with her birth mother just before Christmas. The birth mother and I have been in contact via telephone and email and this reconnection has been unbelievable in a circle of love.

—Connie Hope Diamond
Beaming mother of two adopted daughters

The Answer (to an adopted child)
Not flesh of my flesh
Nor bone of my bone,
But still miraculously
My own.
Never forget
For a single minute:
You didn't grow under my heart
But in it.

— Fleur Conkling Heyliger —

Legacy of an Adopted Child

Once there were two women who never knew each other.
One you do not remember, the other you call Mother.
Two different lives shaped to make you one.
One became your guiding star, the other became your sun.

The first one gave you life, and the second taught you to live it.
The first gave you a need for love. The second was there to give it.

One gave you a nationality. The other gave you a name.
One gave you a talent. The other gave you aim.

One gave you emotions. The other calmed your fears.
One saw your first sweet smile. The other dried your tears.

One sought for you a home that she could not provide.
The other prayed for a child and her hope was not denied.

And now you ask me, through your tears,
the age-old question unanswered through the years.

Heredity or environment, which are you a product of?
Neither, my darling. Neither. Just two different kinds of Love.

— Author Unknown —

Advice

I used to tell my children "Do well, stay well." Then the youngest changed it to "Be well, stay well" and we both grew up.
—Linda Ferber

Parents can only give good advice or put [their children] on the right paths, but the final forming of a person's character lies in their own hands.
—Anne Frank

Always be a first-rate version of yourself,
instead of a second-rate version of somebody else.
—Judy Garland

You are unique, and if that is not fulfilled,
then something wonderful has been lost.
—Martha Graham

I always had three rules when raising my daughter . . .
1) to know her friends well;
2) to choose battles wisely;
3) to treat her with respect.

—Debra Simpson, www.DebraSimpson.com

Don't back down just to keep the peace.
Standing up for your beliefs builds self-confidence and self-esteem.
—Oprah Winfrey

From a Nana to Seven Grandchildren

* A fresh diet of fruits and veggies bring me more peace and calm.
I do what I eat.
* I am young, but naturally intelligent, so I can understand some of
the big issues affecting my life.
* I don't need all the material things that are displayed on TV. In fact,
I don't need TV.
* That my sensations of anger, and negative circumstances are never
permanent.
My intensity of feelings vary from moment to moment in time.
* I only want love and real attention from my family.

Speak to us of Children

And a woman who held a babe against her bosom said,
"Speak to us of Children."

And he said:
"Your children are not your children.
They are the sons and daughters of Life's longing for itself.
They come through you but not from you,
And though they are with you, yet they belong not to you.

You may give them your love but not your thoughts.
For they have their own thoughts.
You may house their bodies but not their souls,
For their souls dwell in the house of tomorrow, which you cannot
visit, not even in your dreams.

You may strive to be like them, but seek not to make them like you.
For life goes not backward nor tarries with yesterday.

You are the bows from which your children as living arrows are sent
forth. The archer sees the mark upon the path of the infinite, and He
bends you with His might that His arrows may go swift and far.
Let your bending in the archer's hand be for gladness;

For even as he loves the arrow that flies,
so He loves also the bow that is stable."
—Kahlil Gibran

A Mother's Intuition

Trust your hunches. They're usually based on facts filed away just below the conscious level.
—Dr. Joyce Brothers, psychologist and television personality

Every time you don't follow your inner guidance, you feel a loss of energy, loss of power, a sense of spiritual deadness.
—Shakti Gawain

Hunch. Gut feeling. Voice of God. Instinct. Many names. One Force.
—Cath Kachur, Speaker, Artist, www.HumanTuneUp.com

Women don't listen to the voice inside them.
We get our lives so busy—it [intuition] is a gift from God.
—Marie Osmond, singer, actress, celebrity mother, on *Oprah*

Listen to your intuition, for it is your best friend,
Ignore your fears, for they are your enemy,
Believe in your dreams, for they are your future.
—Barbara Sanfilippo, Speaker, Author *Dream Big! What's the Best That Can Happen* www.Barbara-Sanfilippo.com

From the moment Eve took a bite of that fruit from the tree in the middle of the garden, just as she was promised, her eyes were opened and she did indeed gain the knowledge of good and evil. It's called women's intuition and it has been passed down from generation to generation for thousands of years. In some cultures it is revered, in others condemned and feared. But one thing has remained constant down through the decades—every woman knows that she has it.
© 2005 Joni Wilson. All Rights Reserved. Reprinted with Permission.
From Thunder Behind the Silence: When a Woman Finds Her Voice
— Joni Wilson, Speaker, Singer, Voice Expert, Author, JoniWilsonVoice.com

Follow your instincts. That's where true wisdom manifests itself.
—Oprah Winfrey

A Mother's Love

Maternal Love:
A miraculous substance which God multiplies as He divides it.
—Victor Hugo

Look into my eyes and hear what I'm not saying,
for my eyes speak louder than my voice ever will.
—Marielou S. Florendo

Some people think that it's holding on that makes one strong;
sometimes it's letting go.
—Unknown

PRECIOUS CHILD.... A MOTHER'S LOVE

Precious child come here by me,
Your precious face I want to see,
Your mama is ill and can't stay long,
Precious child we must be strong.

Mama loves you oh so much,
Take my hand I need your touch.
Let me hold you near my heart,
Precious child we soon must part.

Remember I love you and will always be near,
In memories we've made that you can hold dear.
The hardest thing that I must do,
Is leave my beautiful life with you.

You've blessed my life with love and joy,
You're a precious child and my little boy.
The moment has come and I must go,
Precious child I love you so!

— Judith A. Duran —

A Woman's Wisdom

See yourself in everything because everything is already within you.
—Cynthia Brian, speaker, radio and TV show host
Author *Chicken Soup for the Gardener's Soul*
www.BeTheStarYouAre.org

The flower of a woman's wisdom blooms within her heart.
—Laurel Burch, Artist *Celebrating the Heart of Womankind*

Never mistake knowledge for wisdom.
One helps you make a living; the other helps you make a life.
—Sandra Carey

Don't compromise yourself. You are all you've got.
—Janis Joplin

A woman is the full circle.
Within her is the power to create, nurture, and transform.
—Diane Mariechild

How wrong it is for a woman to expect the man to build the world
she wants, rather than to create it herself.
—Anais Nin

I am a woman above everything else.
—Jacqueline Bouvier Kennedy Onassis

Life on the planet is born of woman.
—Adrienne Rich

Babies

Cherub

Cherub you are, with little
porcelain hand wrapped
around extended finger.
Eyelashes cover virgin eyes
to a world in which I shelter you ~
You are still an innocent
as sweet as the pink blossom
on your newly formed lips.
Perfect are your features,
and pore less is your skin.
Did you fall from heaven -
my precious white winged angel?
Where do you hide your wings?
I swaddle you in Mother's arms
never wanting this moment's end.

—Lee A. Barron, Publisher, Author
Copyright © 2004 Lee A. Barron

Father asked us what was God's noblest work.
Anna said men, but I said babies.
Men are often bad, but babies never are.
—Louisa May Alcott

Those who say they "sleep like a baby" haven't got one.
—A new mother

Giving birth is like taking your lower lip and forcing it over your head.
—Carol Burnett

A baby is born with a need to be loved - and never outgrows it.
—Frank A. Clark

It was the tiniest thing I ever decided to put my whole life into.
—Terri Guillemets

Babies are necessary to grown-ups.
A new baby is like the beginning of all things —
wonder, hope, a dream of possibilities.
In a world that is cutting down its trees to build highways,
losing its earth to concrete... babies are almost the only remaining
link with nature, with the natural world of living things from which
we spring.
—Eda J. Le Shan

No animal is so inexhaustible as an excited infant.
—Amy Leslie

My obstetrician was so dumb that when I gave birth he forgot
to cut the cord. For a year that kid followed me everywhere.
It was like having a dog on a leash.
—Joan Rivers

A baby is God's opinion that the world should go on.
—Carl Sandburg

A baby is a blank cheque made payable to the human race.
—Barbara Christine Seifert

It sometimes happens, even in the best of families, that a baby is
born. This is not necessarily cause for alarm. The important thing
is to keep your wits about you and borrow some money.
—Elinor Goulding Smith

A baby is an angel whose wings decrease as his legs increase.
—Unknown

Sign posted on a Maternity Room door:
"Push. Push. Push."

CAUGHT BY THE ITALIAN GRANDPARENTS

I have a very busy life as an Obstetrician Gynecologist. The days are never boring because, despite our best efforts to create a manageable schedule, the unexpected often occurs. I had been caring for a wonderful couple, Luisa and Bill, throughout their first pregnancy. She was Italian and he an American. We had established an especially warm rapport so I wasn't surprised when Luisa said her parents had just arrived from Italy, had come to hear the baby's heartbeat and wanted to meet me.

It was already one of THOSE days. I was running behind, trying to give everyone everything they needed and didn't have the time for ANYTHING extra. But I knew how important this was for all of them and with my full mastery of the Italian language amounting to "Ciao and grande" I went into the room and said, "Buenos Dais." Introductions of Anastasia and Luigi were made, I smiled and bowed and worried about the time. They were all thrilled, I was happy I took the time. Luisa's mother said," Arrivederci," and I was off to the next room and never looked back. The whole event receded into the background and I forgot all about it.

About a week later, I was again in the middle of office hours, when we received the call from Labor & Delivery that Luisa was in active labor, surely soon to deliver. I apologized to the patient I was presently interviewing; yelled to my nurse that I was on my way; hoofed it across the parking lot, rushed up the back stairs, through the waiting room and only then slowed my step and entered Room One saying calmly, "Looks like today is THE day!"

The nurses were preparing equipment; Luisa was writhing and yelling in bed; her husband was coaching ,"Relax, relax !!!!!"; the TV was blaring; the intercom outside was paging for Dr. Smith to Room Four; there was screaming from the labor room next door.

Calmly talking to Luisa, while examining her, it was obvious that it was time for her to push the baby down. I gave her instructions; reviewed with her husband, the coach; and told her the nurse would help her while I went to change my clothes.

I walked out of the room then flew down the hallway; through the waiting room; into the locker room, grabbing scrubs; quickly changed; raced back down the hall through the waiting room; and stepped into Room One. She was pushing calmly and effectively and within 20 minutes the baby was born.

The cord was cut by Bill; the baby and both parents were crying; there were orders for suture and pain medication; blood loss was estimated; pediatrician called; footprints printed on the birth certificate and Bill's shirt.

Luisa was cleaned up and settled in bed. The infant was given to Luisa, swaddled and she settled down to breast feed like a pro. They thanked me profusely for being so helpful and calm, encouraging and in control and helping them so that there were no problems. Their special gift to me was the naming of the baby Rene Carolina. None of my babies, in 20 years of practice has ever been named anything like Carol.

I went out of the room and flew back down the hall; back to my office to fall back into the originally scheduled flow of patients and to see what my nurse had done with those who suddenly were bumped by this unpredicted birthday party.

Bill and Luisa later told me that I had them totally fooled about what was going on that day since all they had witnessed was my behavior when I was with them. I had responded to them like they were my only concern that day; that I was totally focused and calm. But her parents had been in the waiting room the whole time and had witnessed the hustle and urgency with which I moved outside of Labor Room One. As Billy Crystal said, "It doesn't matter how you feel. It only matters how you look. And you looked, marvelous!"

—Carol Grabowski

HOUSE RULES

If you sleep on it......... make it up.
If you wear it.............. hang it up.
If you drop it................pick it up.
If you eat off it............. wash it.
If you open it............... close it.
If you turn it on........... turn it off.
If you empty it............. fill it.
If it rings...................... answer it.
If it howls....................feed it.
If it cries....................... love it.

Being a Mother

I didn't know I was capable of feeling so much emotion before I was a mother. I had never known the warmth, the joy, the love, the heartache, the miracle, the wonderment or the immense satisfaction of being a mom. Yet being a mother is the most important, yet under-rated job that I'll ever have. No amount of money, no prestige or grand title, and no lauds of recognition anyone could bestow upon me is more valuable than to hear my young daughter say she loves me when I tuck her in. Or see her drop everything and run to me with arms widespread when I arrive to pick her up from preschool. Or feel her wrap her arms around me and give me an unsolicited hug. I get gloriously happy over her simple grin.

Everything I do, whether in work, at play, or around the house, is for the benefit of my child. I never thought I could be so unselfish with my time, energy, attention and affection. But here I am, almost five years since learning that I was blessed to be pregnant at age 43. Although I was in reasonably good health and physical condition, my husband and I were worried that there might be something "not right," due to my age. But she was "perfect."

I endured nine months of chronic nausea, frequent discomfort (including all the poking, prodding, two doses of sickeningly sweet syrup, and an extremely long amniocentesis needle, not to mention the sore back, hips and feet or the scar from the C-section), frequent schedule changes, and an enormous amount of fatigue. Yet, I would do it all over again in a heartbeat for another child.

Before my daughter was born, I never knew that something so small and precious could affect my life so dramatically. I didn't know that a baby could make me feel so important and happy. I never knew that I could love someone so much. After she was born, I held her to my breast and nursed her for 5 months, then gently cradled her head while placing her in her crib. Before I was a mom, I had never held a sleeping baby just because I didn't want to put her down. And now, to this day, I still rock with her before she sleeps at night (usually to read a story, but sometimes just to cuddle), even though she's certainly old enough to get into bed by herself at this point.

Before I was a mom, I didn't know the feeling of having my heart outside my body. A few months ago, however, my young daughter placed her hands over her chest, and said, "My heart's in here,

Mommy." I choked back tears as I placed my hands over my chest and replied, "Yes, baby, your heart's in here."

Before I was a mom, I had never felt what it was like to have my heart break into a million tiny pieces when I couldn't stop her hurt. I had never looked into teary eyes and cried myself. I was the one who cried when I held her down so that her nurses could give her shots. I taught her to pray before meals, play nicely, say "please" and "thank you," be patient (do you have any idea how difficult it is for a 2-year-old to wait, even for a minute), to eat with a fork and spoon, to love the outdoors, the difference between a bathtub and a pool, to sing "Happy Birthday," and so much more. She absorbed all of it, and is now a beautiful, happy, articulate, opinionated 4-year-old.

It's so difficult not to spoil her. However, I know that to grow into a loving, confident, cooperative adult, she needs discipline tempered with love; safety and security couched in encouragement and exploration; answers surrounded by more questions; faith nestled in tolerance; and so much more. I have only a short time to give her all of this, and I will spend every waking moment of that time being her mother. It's an awesome responsibility, one that I take seriously and eagerly. I never knew I would love being a Mother.

—Sharon M. McCarthy, Megan's mom
Reprinted with permission from *Heart of A Woman*

TWINS

Most people think "WOW you must have your hands full!"
Yes, that is true. It can be a bit of a roller coaster at times but it's the best ride I have ever been on. I don't look at it as work - I look at it as a double blessing. I can't imagine it any other way! Having Twins is the most wonderful thing I have ever experienced. Everything from the attention you get from total strangers every time you eat out, to seeing them interact together and knowing they will have a bond no one else can understand.

The benefits of twins are endless and I feel overwhelmed with joy that I was given the opportunity to experience this wonderful gift. Twins may be double the trouble, but they are also double the joy.

—Tiffany Altman Chernault

Challenges

How easily Nature overcomes every obstacle.
Like Nature, we should adapt to life's circumstances,
overcoming them with patience and enthusiasm.
—Amma (Mother), Mata Amritanandamayi, India
Messages from Amma: In the Language of the Heart, www.amma.org

No human being is immune to adversity or personal setbacks.
—Hillary Rodham Clinton

You don't develop courage by being happy in your relationships
everyday. You develop it by surviving difficult times and challenging
adversity.
—Barbara De Angelis

Our difficulties in life call us to go deeper within ourselves.
Our challenges force us to develop better skills, more abilities,
and new ways of thinking, doing and being.
They draw forth a greater strength and deeper wisdom
from our inner selves.
—Peggy O'Neill, Speaker, Author *Walking Tall: Overcoming Inner
Smallness No Matter What Size You Are* www.YoPeggy.com

Life's challenges are not supposed to paralyze you,
they're supposed to help you discover who you are.
—Bernice Johnson Reagon

You gain strength, courage and confidence by every experience
in which you really stop to look fear in the face. You are able to
say to yourself, "I lived through this horror. I can take the next thing
that comes along." . . . You must do the thing you think you cannot do.
—Eleanor Roosevelt

No matter how much you're struggling today,
always look to tomorrow.
Then you will look back and realize you can always,
manage whatever life brings you.
—Joanne Roush

The difference between stumbling blocks and stepping stones
is how you use them.
—Unknown

Always continue the climb.
It is possible for you to do whatever you choose,
if you first get to know who you are and are willing to work
with a power that is greater than ourselves to do it.
—Oprah Winfrey

Pushing Boundaries

Being Karen's mother was always a challenge. She pushed the
boundaries to their limit. When she was a teenager, she and her
boy-friend and another couple went to a movie in a neighboring
town. I told her to be home by 11:00 o'clock because she'd been
out late several times that week. Her father and I went to bed and
must have dozed off, because 11:00 o'clock came and went and
Karen still wasn't home.

Imagine my surprise when at 11:30, there were 4 teenagers
standing at the foot of our bed, as Karen explained that it wasn't
her fault she was late. The movie didn't end until after 11:00 and
her companions would not leave until it was over.

She was furious with them. When they brought her home, one of
the boys said, "Boy am I glad I don't have to face your parents."

To that, Karen replied, "Ha! You got me in trouble and you aren't
leaving until you explain to my parents," and marched them all
inside.

Karen is still challenging the world, and doing quite a job of it!
I never worried about people taking advantage of her. She can
hold her own.

—Garnet Brassfield, Mother of Karen Robertson (who went on to
write *Raising Kids Right*)

Strong-Willed Young Daughters

Raising a strong-willed daughter had its challenges. Jodi (10) was so much like me. One evening, I walked into her bedroom. We had been butting heads all day long, and it was time to make amends, hug, and make-up.

Unfortunately, she wasn't ready to call a truce and her demeanor said so. I talked to her calmly and hoped that the whole situation would be quelled and we'd end the day at peace. She, on the other hand, had no such idea.

"I love you so much, Jodi." I waited for her to respond in kind, but she stared at the ceiling. I hugged her as she lay like a post in the bed with her arms straight down at her sides. She continued to stare coldly at the ceiling.

I yearned for her to throw her arms around my neck and tell me she loved me, too. But Jodi lay motionless and unresponsive. She was tough. Even though my heart was breaking, I got up from the bed, turned, walked from the room, closed the door, and left her in the dark alone.

Tears came to my eyes as I walked through the house and straight to my bathroom where I could cry without being heard. I quickly shed my clothes and got into the shower as the sobs began.
Dear God, please help me with Jodi. Please soften her heart toward me.

Suddenly, with no warning, the shower curtain was ripped back and there stood Jodi, tears running down her face. "I love you, too, Mom." And she disappeared out of the room.
Thank you, Lord.

—Karen Robertson, Author of *Raising Kids Right*,
www.giantstepsuccess.com

Childhood Dreams

OUT OF THE PINEY WOODS

Can you remember a time when you went to school feeling depressed and without an ounce of self-esteem? Can you remember the teacher who told you how special you were and helped you see you are important? I will introduce you to one of those teachers who grew up wanting to help children.

My Mother was born March 4, 1916, in Fisher, Louisiana. Woodrow Wilson was President of the United States, a loaf of bread cost 7 cents, milk cost 36 cents a gallon, gas was 23 cents a gallon and you could mail a letter for 2 cents.

Fisher was a small village, the last of the old sawmill towns during the golden age of lumbering in Western Louisiana. The village had an interdenominational church, a depot, a hotel, a hospital and schools. The lumber company employed two capable physicians to supply the medical needs of its employees.

My Mother was five years old when she started to school. When asked what she wanted to be when she grew up she said, "All I ever wanted to be was a school teacher." After going to school all day my Mother and some of the other children would meet in the back of the two story school house and play school on the back steps.

High School? She was valedictorian of her graduating class. She received a scholarship to attend Louisiana State Normal College for tuition, but not room and board and books. Everyone told her she might as well forget it. She would not be able to attend college. Her family had no extra money for the young girl who had her heart set on becoming a teacher. However, she did not give up on her dream. Becoming a teacher would make it possible for her to leave the piney woods and live a better life and would never have to go hungry again.

Many days she went to classes hungry, with holes in her stockings. Instead of buying textbooks, she went to the library and studied there.

Two years later she started a career that spanned over thirty years of influencing and teaching children to be good citizens. Unknown numbers of children of all ages have received her creative and innovative teaching. Her own daughter niece became teachers because of her influence. Her three children all received a college education. There is no way to tell how many children she challenged and influenced to become productive citizens.

Many others might have given up on becoming a teacher during the Depression. Money was scarce and it was not easy to do without to get an education. But she realized early that she wanted to be a teacher and spent her life working hard to help those around her no matter their age.

What a legacy to leave behind in the world, hundreds of children and adults, who are better for being in a class taught by my Mother.

On the occasion of her ninetieth birthday some of those that she has influenced shared their feelings:

From her son: "Thank you for something that you may not have realized and that is the confident attitude that you instilled in your children. As I reflect back on your influence on me, I can always remember that you were a doer. You were always involved and taking the lead whether it was PTA, school or church. You showed by your actions an air of confidence and that was a great example. You always supported and encouraged anything I tried."

From her daughter: "Thank you so much for teaching us the gospel and most of all for being a good example. Thank you for always being there."

From a Toastmaster friend: "I remember being so impressed that you went on a mission for your church after retirement. In some way you probably motivated me to join the Peace Corps in my late fifties."

From a grandson: "You always had the spirit of adventure-a fact that you demonstrated more than once on the trips we shared."

From a daughter: "One of the best traits you taught me was that I could do anything because you just lived the fact that you could do anything. You left the piney woods and became a teacher. You wanted to teach school and you just DID IT. Whatever it took, you were willing to do it to reach your goal."

—Billie J. Jones

Dedicated to Lola Jordan, Mother, Grandmother, Great-grandmother, friend, and teacher, we appreciate you and are glad you have touched our lives forever.

Children

Children's talent to endure stems from their ignorance of alternatives.
—Maya Angelou, Author *I Know Why the Caged Bird Sings*, 1969

Children are like flowers, nurture them
and they will grow up strong and beautiful.
—Lydia Boyd, Past International Director, Toastmasters International

If our American way of life fails the child, it fails us all.
—Pearl S. Buck

Gray hair is God's graffiti.
—Bill Cosby

Cleaning your house while your kids are still growing up
is like shoveling the walk before it stops snowing.
—Phyllis Diller

Life, love, and laughter—what priceless gifts to give our children.
—Phyllis Dryden

There was never a child so lovely
but his mother was glad to get him to sleep.
—Ralph Waldo Emerson

I believe that children are our future.
Teach them well and let them lead the way.
Show them all the beauty they possess inside.
—Whitney Houston, Mother, Singer, Actress

Mama exhorted her children at every opportunity to
'jump at de sun.' We might not land on the sun,
but at least we would get off the ground.
—Zora Neale Hurston

Think what a better world it would be if we all, the whole world, had cookies and milk about three o'clock every afternoon and then lay down on our blankets for a nap.
—Barbara Jordan

The real menace in dealing with a five-year-old
is that in no time at all you begin to sound like a five-year-old.
—Joan Kerr, *Please Don't Eat the Daisies*, 1957

My daughter McKaley was about 4 and was always in a good mood. I asked her one night before bed how she was able to always be happy. She told me that it was very easy. "All you have to do is go to bed smiling and you will automatically wake up happy." I asked her how she makes sure that she is always smiling at bed time. McKaley replied, "I just look out my bedroom window and remember when you told me that all of the stars are shining especially for me"!
—Erin King

Women gather together to wear silly hats, eat dainty food, and forget how unresponsive their husbands are. Men gather to talk sports, eat heavy food, and forget how demanding their wives are. Only where children gather is there any real chance of fun.
—Mignon McLaughlin

No matter how old a mother is, she watches her middle-aged children for signs of improvement.
—Florida Scott-Maxwell

Children are one third of our population and all of our future.
—Select Panel for the Promotion of Child Health, 1981

Children desperately need to know - and to hear in ways they understand and remember - that they're loved and valued by mom and dad.
—Paul Smally

Parents learn a lot from their children about coping with life.
—Muriel Spark

Each day of our lives we make deposits
in the memory banks of our children.
—Charles R. Swindoll

The very young do not always do as they are told.
—The Nox (Armin Shimmerman actor), TV Series *Stargate SG:1*

We worry about what a child will become tomorrow,
yet we forget that (s)he is someone today.
—Stacia Tauscher

If I were a caterpillar I would like to hang out on a wall where
little children gather to talk about life and love so that I would
be able to have colorful words of wisdom to take with me on
my upcoming journey.
—Catherine Tilley, www.theglobalvoice.com

If you have a lot of tension and you get a headache,
do what it says on the aspirin bottle:
"Take two aspirin" and "Keep away from children."
—Unknown

A child can ask questions that a wise man cannot answer.
—Unknown

One hundred years from now it will not matter what your bank
account was, the sort of house you lived in, or the kind of car you
drove...but the world may be different because YOU were important
in the life of a child.
—Unknown

Children seldom misquote. In fact, they usually repeat word for word
what you shouldn't have said.
—Unknown

Children are the living messages we send to a time we will not see.
—John W. Whitehead, *The Stealing of America*, 1983

THE LIGHTER SIDE OF RAISING CHILDREN:

You spend the first two years of their life teaching them
to walk and talk. Then you spend the next sixteen telling
them to sit down and shut up.

Grandchildren are God's reward for not killing your own children.

Children seldom misquote you.
In fact, they usually repeat word for word
of what you shouldn't have said.

The main purpose of holding children's parties is to remind yourself
that there are children more awful than your own.

We child-proofed our homes, but they are still getting in.

Dear Mr. God,
I wish you would not make it so easy for people to come apart.
I had to have 3 stitches and a shot.
—Janet, *Kid's Theology*

When my twin daughters were young, I taught them to say a prayer
before going to bed. As I listened outside their door, I could hear
them say "Give us this steak and daily bread, and forgive us our
mattresses." My husband and I always had a good laugh over this.
That was over 50 years ago, and the memory remains in my heart.

I remember thinking a prayer was "Give us this day our jelly bread."

My son, who is in nursery school, said, "Our Father, who art in
Heaven, how didja know my name?"

ADVICE FOR THE DAY:

Be nice to your kids . . .
for one day they will choose your nursing home.

THEY SAY THE DARN'DEST THINGS...

When my daughter, Halihannah, was 3 years old we were getting into the car to drive to my sister's house for a Memorial Day Bar-B-Que. Halihannah said to wait and got out of her car seat. She said she needed to get memorial out of the house. My husband and I just looked at each other a bit puzzled but she was on a mission..so he unlocked the house door and she went in. She came back and announced that she had memorial and was ready to go. Once I got her back into the car seat she showed me her beanie baby, Moray the Moray Eel. Memorial day to her meant "my moray eel day."

When she was 4, our friends who had a son, Stephen, three days after we had our first daughter joined us for dinner in a restaurant. The adults were talking while the kids were interested in going under the table. Halihannah came up chewing gum. I did not know she knew what the stuff was, let alone what to do with it. I asked her where she got the gum and she said under the table and that there was more and offered me some. Stephen said "This is the best–having all this gum to choose from. If you don't like one flavor of one, then just take another piece!"

—Patty Anderson

Fairy Clock

There's a wonderful clock upon our shelf,
Numbered in fairies from one to twelve,
Dressed in colors bright and gay,
They circle around as it ticks away,
One by one they skip and run
Over the hands, Oh what fun.
The king and queen, a beautiful sight,
In tiny jewels that sparkle at night,
Wouldn't you like to see for yourself,
This wonderful clock upon our shelf?

— Rose Kawa Stern —
Written at Age 10

Mother of Blanche Katz

Daughters

Lessons Learned from My Daughter:
* Not all birds die when rescued and put in a box.
* Laundry can be done every two weeks if one has enough clothing and underwear.
* Books are to be read in the bathtub.
* Why do today what can be put off until midnight.
* Not all shy children stay that way.
* There is strength in being tall and beautiful.
* Food should be fast and tasty.
* Why drink water when one can slurp an icee.
* Small children and little sisters are extremely annoying.
* Large garden caterpillars are actually tomorrow's' butterflies.
* There's no such thing as having too many stuffed animals.
* Closets should be properly organized using plastic containers and color-coded hangers.
* Some children become athletic in high school.
* There is strength in being quiet and gentle.
* Anyone can be suspect in stealing a chicken.
* Only your little sister can be suspect when something is missing around the house.
* Respect can be earned without being loud and pushy.
* One can never read too many books.
* Bed sheets need never be changed;
  they always work the way they are.
* Vacuuming is optional as well.
* Forget cleaning sinks and toilets while we're at it.
* Spare time should be spent reading, not cleaning.
* Some children are admired by many people for helping and doing wonderful things that you'll never know about.
* There's no such thing as overfeeding a chicken.
* One can never see too many movies.
* One can never have too many cats.
* One can never have too much clothing.
* One can love a chicken.

—Mary Gay Roush, RN, mother of two daughters
"Things I've Learned from Serina"

MY IRIS GAYLE

My Iris Gale is quite a girl
For her each night I knit and purl,
And sit and wonder with furrowed brow,
If it is possible, and why and how.

Her little form stirs in my heart,
A love that words cannot impart.
The thought of her makes my heart leap.
I can't believe she's mine to keep.

She has a pert little turned up nose,
With a darling mouth like a pink tea rose.
And when she smiles her face lights up
Like the morning sun on a buttercup.

Then when into her room I creep,
To watch as she smiles in her sleep,
I know that nothing can replace
The love I feel for my angel face.

Yes, Iris Gayle is quite a girl
For her each night I knit and purl,
And sit and wonder with furrowed brow,
If it is possible and why and how.

—Rosalie Ferrer Kramer, Speaker, Poet, Author—
Dancing in the Dark: Things My Mother Never Told Me

I Feel So Blessed

When I was diagnosed with cancer, that day my life changed in so many ways; I was able to see through a new pair of glasses... My stay in the hospital was long, but I was never alone. My husband and two daughters took shifts around the clock staying with me, I knew in my heart God was with me but sometimes it sure helps to have someone with skin on them there... I was in total awe watching my daughters. Two loving compassionate women, with strength and courage... I know as a Mother we doubt ourselves at times. Was I a good enough mother? Did I do anything right?I should have done it better... you know all that self-talk we can do to ourselves. Well, I knew at that moment, without a doubt, that I had done something right. What a gift from something so frightening, came the knowing that everything is just as it should be and I knew from my heart I would look at them differently, with respect of the women they are and the gifts they not only have to give for their own families but to the world... I feel so Blessed.
—Sandra Nash

To My Daughter, Who Has Been My Life's Reward

Through the years I watched you grow, change and forever seek answers to the miracle of life.

The happiest moments of my life were the hours, days and years we spent together.

At times, when you were little, I had the overwhelming desire to hold you close to keep you safe from ever experiencing the transitions of life. I soon realized that I needed to let go.

Each transition was difficult for me...your first day in kindergarten; putting you on a school bus to a school many miles from home; accepting your High School years when our mother-daughter relationship was tested in all areas.

Then the divorce...which left you feeling lost, hurt and torn between the conflicts of two parents that you loved.

Saying good-bye to you as you drove off to college in another state. This was the saddest moment of my life, knowing that this was the pivotal point for you to experience living away from home. And for me, the realization that you would probably never again live at home.

You made me so proud with every turn of your life, especially going from undergraduate school to getting your Masters.

You, my beautiful and very accomplished daughter, set your goals high and higher. You reached for the stars and they responded.

You were not without disappointments during your 20's and early 30's. But you faced each challenge with determination, optimism and inner strength.

I am so blessed that you choose me to give you life on earth and now you have been blessed with a gift from God–a baby boy named Dominic whose soul has selected you and Brian to nurture and love from newborn to beyond.

You will experience the joys I felt throughout the years' of raising you to this gorgeous, talented and loving daughter.

My dearest one, I love our mother-daughter relationship and best of all I love being best friends.

Loving you forever, Mom
—Beverly Stubbs Weurding

A Daughter's Inspiration

My 19 year-old daughter took a semester off from college and thur-hiked the entire length of the Appalachian Trail (2,160 miles) by herself. This grueling trek extends from Springer Mountain, Georgia to Mount Katadin, Maine and includes hiking over treacherous terrain through all kinds of weather carrying all of your supplies in a 50-pound backpack. As her mother I was petrified of what might happen to her and yet supported her need to prove she could handle this tremendous physical and mental challenge.

Her successful completion of this feat–after four months of fighting blisters, black flies, and aching joints–was celebrated by her family and friends, and inspired me to look for something to stretch myself. I had been running three miles several times a week to try and stay in shape but had never considered going beyond that, actually thought I was too old to do much more.

However, encouraged by my daughter's recent challenging accomplishment, I decided to celebrate my 50th birthday by participating in a mini-marathon running event, a distance of 13.1 miles. I trained for the race for four months and there were many times I wanted to quit, especially when my knees hurt and the temperature was well below freezing. I would remember what my daughter had faced and how she refused to give up on her goal.

I did participate in and finish the mini-marathon event and while not setting any land speed records, everyone in my family celebrated with me as I crossed the finish line. I know as moms we are role models for our children and constantly encourage them to set goals and achieve them. I am proud to say that children can sometimes do the same for us!

—Debby Pratt

Mother-Daughter Connection
...the great strength of women. We are connected throughout time and regardless of place. We are our mother's daughters.

—Cokie Roberts, Author *We Are Our Mother's Daughters*
Mother, ABC's chief congressional analyst
whose own mother, Lindy Boggs, was a Congresswoman

A loving and careful mother both recognizes and even protects her daughter's autonomy and also helps her dance out confidently on to a wider stage.
—Rachel Billington, From *The Great Umbilical*

I tell my daughter all the time "no matter what you do, I will always love you. No matter how old you are, you will always be my baby. No matter how big you are, you can always get a time out.
—Effie Horning, Mother of two adopted children

A daughter is a mother's gender partner, her closest ally in the family confederacy, an extension of her self. And mothers are their daughters' role model, their biological and emotional road map, the arbiter of all their relationships.
—Victoria Secunda

The little girl dances to the song of love in the grown ups heart.
—Catherine Tilley, Founder of the Institute for Global Healing

Teapots and Teacups
Teapots and teacups,
Mothers and daughters,
Creating warmth.
At times steaming
Other times cool.
Pouring in and filling up,
Cherished moments.
Drinking in nourishment,
Sometimes bitter,
Sometimes sweet.
Always permeated with love,
Refreshing, relaxing.
Giving comfort and encouragement,
Sharing secrets,
Celebrating life,
In big and small ways.
Treasuring memories,
Embracing the spirit,
Renewing the soul.

— Julie Tungate Moses —
To my mom on Mother's Day 2004 and read at her funeral May 2006

Dear Mom

Dear Mom,

Hi! It's me again. Just wanted to write a little something to let you know how great you are. Where do I even begin? I tell all my friends that I have been so blessed to have had the upbringing that I did. To grow up in a home where I never felt unloved and there was always laughter I am so grateful that I grew up where my parents loved and honored each other and modeled what a godly relationship looks like. I look at some of the people I know and even society as a whole and not everyone likes their mom, shoot their dads too. I am so lucky to not only love you because you are my mom, but love you because you are my friend. That is pretty cool.

Looking back on all my 24 years of life... there isn't a time that I can remember that you have ever let me down. Thank you for that. When I see you I see a woman that is tough yet gentle. It makes my giggle to hear dad tell stories of how you used to be (reserved I guess would be the best word to describe you then). I see you now and you are very vocal and I love that. People look up to you and admire you (me being one of them). You speak your mind and when you feel that there is an injustice you don't just complain or talk about it... you write letters and attempt to right some wrongs. Mom you have got so much spunk and personality and I am so glad that I have gotten some of that too.

You don't always tell me what to do, but you have showed me what to do by living your life. You have modeled for me how I aspire to be (all of your imperfections included... let's be honest no one is perfect as much as we like to joke that we are). My spirit is joyful when I am around you. Geez, when we get together and start joking and laughing those are my favorite memories. It is funny that dad and Kenon <brother> just let us be when that happens.

Mom I just love you so much. For all your hugs and kisses.
And even your times of discipline. Thank you for being true to yourself so I know how to be true to myself. I love you.
Love,
Me

—Jessica Nibbs

Dinner Time

The Banquet

Twelve starving, rambunctious people all expecting dinner to
be served, NOW!!!!!! The kitchen a mere 8x8 foot affair.
No fancy appliances, foods, butler, or maid! No dishwasher!

Sounds like a cook's worst nightmare. But no, this was dinner at
our house every day. Orchestrated by my parents using creativity
and love to fill in the deficits of resources as they raised their
TEN children.

Bluebird blue with white spots, Melmac dinner ware, (lifetime,
no breakage guarantee) graced that table. There were no glasses
on that table, so as to never spoiling ones' dinner with too much
drink, but really to avoid spills. Practically every meal included the
big yellow bowl (one gallon size), holding just the right amount
of tossed salad, macaroni and cheese, spaghetti, tuna noodle
casserole, rice pudding to feed that crowd. The correct amount
of potatoes was guaranteed by filling the pressure cooker to the
brim and then watching that they didn't boil over. Dessert was
often bread and jam. Milk was always in gallon jugs.
Leftovers? Unheard of!

Seating all those little butts at one table, brought out the genius in
my creative father. All the table leaves were used, creating a very
long dining room table. He made a 6 1/2 foot, double thick board to
lie across two chairs placed at the ends of one side of the table.
Voila! Instant bench! Seating for six! Four chair legs on each end,
with 12 little legs dangling in between. You won't see anything like
it except with a long row of birds on a wire.

The creativity didn't end there. "The board" was a cumbersome
dining room accoutrement, demanding its own space. My dad
thought of everything! He had attached metal eyes to the edge of
that board and hooks to the underside of the table. The board was
stored between meals, hanging on the side of the table. That
eliminated the need to move that awkward monstrosity any
distance. An activity which had previously resulted in bruised toes
or battered door jams. And it was right there, ready to go, anytime
the crowd gathered.

After dinner activities had their own format as teams of two took turns clearing the table and washing all those dishes. This could take an excruciatingly long time if the "dryer" watched TV while the "washer" filled the drain board with clean dishes and then came back and dried those dishes while the "washer" watched TV. The process could last through *Lassie* AND *The Ed Sullivan Show*. Dad's preference was that we worked together because we would often sing two part harmony while we worked. Mom was just grateful the job was done.

Managing to feed all those hungry mouths was a challenge but those family meals formed the basis of a family spirit which unites all ten children to this day, despite residing as far as 2,400 miles apart. And I feel my mother continues, in heaven, to serve "the banquet of the Lord." And doesn't have to do the dishes there either!

—Carol Grabowski

Dinner Time Pranks
Some of my fondest, funniest memories growing up were those quality times shared around the family meals. It was never about the food itself, as Dad was actually a better cook than Mom, but more about the adventures and conversations... okay, practical jokes played on...MOM!   And my Dad is the best at practical jokes. He says it runs in our family... so we all learned from the masters - him and his older brother Jim.

It all started with my father, playing tricks on Mom at meal time. We would all be seated at the table, one of us three kids would say grace, then while Mom would be getting more hot food from the stove, Dad would snitch something from Mom's plate, and place it on his own (or on ours), to see if she would notice. Sometimes he would distract her to look at something in the opposite direction, or out the kitchen window for a fantastic sunset... and she would! It would take several snitches before Mom would notice, maybe she knew all along, and just played us for the naive ones!

—Sheryl Roush

Dedicated to parents Hiram and Beverly, and brothers Rick and Steve

Do It Anyway

People are often unreasonable, illogical, and self-centered;
Forgive them anyway.
If you are kind, people may accuse you of selfish, ulterior motives;
Be kind anyway.
If you are successful you will win some false friends
and true enemies;
Succeed anyway.
If you are honest and frank, people may cheat you;
Be honest and frank anyway.
What you spend years building, someone could destroy overnight;
Build anyway.
If you find serenity and happiness, they may be jealous;
Be happy anyway.
The good you do today, people will often forget tomorrow;
Do good anyway.
Give the world the best you have, and it may never be enough;
Give the world the best you've got anyway.
You see, in the final analysis, it is between you and God;
It was never between you and them anyway.

— Mother Teresa —

Epiphany's Child

Ann was in so much pain, I didn't know what else to do except to offer to be a surrogate mother for her.

AN OLD SENSE OF SELF

Ann longed to be a mother since she was a young girl. In her early forties, she finally met the man of her dreams, Wayne, and married him. On the outer edge of childbearing years, they immediately started to try to conceive a child to start their new family. Four years later after a vasectomy reversal, meticulous timings, temperature readings, other fertility methods, difficulties with adoption, lots of money and time-still no baby.

A woman nearing defeat, Ann reached out to me for help. Despair showed on her face, seeming to have aged her 10 years. She had begun counseling and taking medication for depression. Ann came to me hoping I would validate her decision to give up on her dream of having a child.

THE EPIPHANY

Ann poured out her heart and answered my questions. We discovered the true reason for her pain. "What if God doesn't think I'd be a good mother-and not give me the chance to be one?" This 'what if' was tearing her apart!

Where did she get that belief? Was it Ann's mother who passed away, or some other insensitive, unthinking relative or friend who may have said something to Ann which is typically the cause of negative beliefs?

Quite the contrary. I asked Ann to tell me more about her mother. With a new rush of tears, Ann described her as incredible, and that she "FEARED SHE COULD NEVER MEASURE UP. If she couldn't be a good mother, then how could God (or even an adoption agency) entrust a baby to her care?!"

Having known Ann for years, I reminded her of the wonderful qualities that made her an excellent mother. I would entrust my own children to her care. Although grateful for my faith in her, it wasn't enough. Tears welled up again in her eyes, still unsure she could be a good mother. Her occupation as a neo-natal intensive care unit nurse made her ultra-sensitive to the fragility of life and motherhood.

I frantically searched my mind for a way to support this woman. I could not let her give up on her dream.

I had to personally do something. Anything. Shake her?
I wanted to scream!

Instead my stomach churned and I gasped for air. I blurted out an offer.
. . to be a surrogate mother!

We sobbed in an embrace.

Ann suddenly realized that someone believed in her enough to give her nine+ months of her life, emotions and spirit, family, career, and health. That moment gave birth to the BELIEF that she COULD have a child. . . that she COULD possibly be a good mother.

I sobbed because Ann believed in her dream again-and I knew she was going to have it!

EPIPHANY'S CHILD
We both knew Ann's life would dramatically change from that moment on. The release of this old belief, this major stumbling block, would alleviate the strain on her health. Nothing now stood in the way of having her dream.

To accelerate the manifestation of her dream, I prodded Ann to take the leap into BEing a mother right then at that epiphany moment. She instinctively knew how to do it-her 'inner mother' was aching to come out! I could see that she BEcame 'mother,' from the look in her eyes.

Ann's epiphany was mine too. I was forty-something–"What the heck did I just do?! ? How would my husband and kids react? What would become of my life? What did I really want for my life?"

Deep inside I prayed that I wouldn't have to fulfill on my promise!
I instinctively knew Ann's belief was the ONLY block. Thousands, if not millions of kids are put up for adoption. There had to be ONE little baby in the world for Ann and Wayne.

As life would have it, I was spared having to fulfill my promise.
Several months later, Ann and Wayne were blessed with their dream. . .
a beautiful healthy newborn girl they later adopted.
A child rush-delivered because of an epiphany.

© 2006 Maria Carter, www.fallinlovewithyourlife.com

Faith

Courage and faith go hand-in-hand.
Courage is simply walking through your fear. Acknowledging it, and,
with faith on your side, moving beyond fear's grip.
—Debbie Barnett, Speaker, www.DebbieBarnett.com

Courage is fear that has said its prayers.
—Dorothy Bernard

Faith is like radar that sees through the fog.
—Corrie Ten Boom, *Tramp for the Lord*

Faith is putting all your eggs in God's basket,
then counting your blessings before they hatch.
—Ramona C. Carroll

Lift your sights. Look at the stars, especially when things seem
darkest. Know that there is a higher power in the universe.
You are not alone.
—Jo Condrill, Speaker, Author *Take Charge of Your Life:
Dare to Pursue Your Dreams*, www.goalminds.com

It's the moment you think you can't that you realize you can.
—Celine Dion

Every blade of grass has its angel that bends over it
and whispers, grow, grow.
—*The Talmud*

"Breathe. Let go. And remind yourself that this very moment is the
only one you know you have for sure."
—Oprah Winfrey

Weave in faith and God will find the thread.
—Unknown

ALL IS WELL

Have you seen the sun as it stays up in the sky?

Do you notice the heavens don't crash down?

And the wind as it calls the birds to fly? It's always there

When the moon has reached its place

It doesn't need any glue it hangs on grace

Without a trace of why

Do you think they're tryin' to tell you somethin'

That all is truly well

Do you think the blood pumping in your veins is magic?

Do you think that the breath you breathe believes in you?

When you close your eyes and forget your fear

Do you fly? Carried by the wind lookin' down on your life

Well I think its tryin' to tell you somethin'

That all is truly well

When I die I think that I shall fly somewhere

Where the sun and the moon begin their day

When you look for me I will be there in the sky

Shinin' down on you from the stars in your eyes

Yes I think I'm tryin' to tell you something

That all is truly well–I think I'm tryin' to tell you somethin'

That all is truly well

Family

A HOUSEWIFE'S LAMENT

I've washed many pair's dirty hands.
And cleaned a zillion pots and pans.
I've removed spots from the new beige carpet,
And made endless trips to the super market
I have tripped countless times on a toy in the hall,
And scrubbed the marks from the ivory wall.
Now I'm ready to run or to fly,
To the land where pants are always dry
Where husbands don't come home and say,
"What, darling, did you do today?"

—Rosalie Ferrer Kramer, Speaker, Poet, Author—
Dancing in the Dark: Things My Mother Never Told Me
www.authorsden.com/rosaliefkramer

The family. We were a strange little band of characters trudging
through life sharing diseases and toothpaste, coveting one another's
desserts, hiding shampoo, borrowing money, locking each other out
of our rooms, inflicting pain and kissing to heal it in the same instant,
loving, laughing, defending, and trying to figure out the common
thread that bound us all together.
—Erma Bombeck

Other things may change us, but we start and end with the family.
—Anthony Brandt

When you look at your life, the greatest happinesses
are family happinesses.
—Dr. Joyce Brothers

To us, family means putting your arms around each other
and being there.
—Barbara Bush

Family:
A social unit where the father is concerned with parking space,
the children with outer space, and the mother with closet space.
—Evan Esar

If you ever start feeling like you have the goofiest, craziest,
most dysfunctional family in the world, all you have to do
is go to a state fair. Because five minutes at the fair, you'll be going,
'you know, we're alright. We are dang near royalty.
—Jeff Foxworthy, Comedian

The great gift of family life is to be intimately acquainted with
people you might never even introduce yourself to, had life not
done it for you.
—Kendall Hailey, *The Day I Became an Autodidact*

Where we love is home, home that our feet may leave,
but not our hearts.
—Oliver Wendell Holmes, physician, poet and humorist

Call it a clan, call it a network, call it a tribe, call it a family.
Whatever you call it, whoever you are, you need one.
—Jane Howard-Feldman

The only rock I know that stays steady, the only institution
I know that works is the family.
—Lee Iacocca

The informality of family life is a blessed condition
that allows us to become our best while looking our worst.
—Marge Kennedy

In some families, please is described as the magic word.
In our house, however, it was sorry.
—Margaret Laurence

Family is just accident....
They don't mean to get on your nerves.
They don't even mean to be your family, they just are.
—Marsha Norman

The family unit plays a critical role in our society
and in the training of the generation to come.
—Sandra Day O'Connor

If the family were a fruit, it would be an orange, a circle of sections,
held together but separable - each segment distinct.
—Letty Cottin Pogrebin

I've definitely never had to look very far outside my family
for inspiration. I'm surrounded by unbelievable strength and courage.
Even in very difficult times, there's always been a lot of humor
and laughter.
—Maria Shriver Schwarzenegger, *More* Magazine, May 2004

You don't choose your family.
They are God's gift to you, as you are to them.
—Archbishop Desmond Tutu

Families are like fudge... mostly sweet with a few nuts.
—Unknown

Fathers

Fatherhood is pretending the present you love most
is soap-on-a-rope.
—Bill Cosby

Why are men reluctant to become fathers?
They aren't through being children.
—Cindy Garner

My father used to play with my brother and me in the yard.
Mother would come out and say, "You're tearing up the grass."
"We're not raising grass," Dad would reply. "We're raising boys."
—Harmon Killebrew

Never ask for anything that costs more than five dollars
when your parents are doing taxes.
—Carrol, Age 9, *Kid's Rules for Life*

Don't flush the toilet when your dad's in the shower.
—Lamar, Age 10, *Kid's Rules for Life*

Remember you're never too old to hold your father's hand.
—Molly, Age 11, *Kid's Rules for Life*

It is much easier to become a father than to be one.
—Kent Nerburn, *Letters to My Son: Reflections on Becoming a Man*

There are three stages of a man's life:
He believes in Santa Claus,
he doesn't believe in Santa Claus,
he is Santa Claus.
—Unknown

A father carries pictures where his money used to be.
—Unknown

Feminini-Tea

Tea Prayer

In honour of the feminine force of energy,
I celebrate the femininity of me.
A universe in balance, with stability,
is the home of fertility;
where souls, dreams and spirits grow.
God is all there is and all we know.
From intimacy, tenderness and delicacy
come a strength of knowing,
a strength of being and a strength of purpose.
The Divine Feminine fortifies my goodness,
my Godness and the Goddess of me.
All that I am embodies and
encompasses true femininity,
pure spirituality and total equality.
For all that defines me as female or feminine,
I embody, embrace and express.
I acknowledge the power of creation and give thanks;
gracefully, humbly, and blissfully for my femininity.
I release the concerns and fears
of feminine versus masculine.
With love and acceptance, there are no more tears.
I let God guide and guard the rest of my years.
And so It does, and so It is.

Amen

—Darlene Fahl-Brittian—
Certified Tea Specialist
Sipping Tea - Celebrating Me
www.TakeUpTheCup.com

Forgiveness

Now our hearts are closed buds that harbor anger, jealousy, and selfishness. But when Love flows and washes away the impurities, our hearts will flower and bless the world.
—Amma (Mother), Mata Amritanandamayi, India
Messages from Amma: In the Language of the Heart, www.amma.org

Without forgiveness life is governed by... an endless cycle of resentment and retaliation.
—Roberto Assagioli

Holding on to anger is like grasping a hot coal with the intent of throwing it at someone else; you are the one who gets burned..
—Buddha

Don't let yourself be so angry that you stop loving. Because one day you'll wake up from that anger, and the person you love will be gone.
—From the TV series *Dawson's Creek*

You cannot please everyone.
The sooner you get this, the better off you'll be.
—Cath Kachur, Speaker, Artist

Forgiveness is the final form of love.
—Reinhold Niebuhr, American theologian, 1892-1971

The practice of forgiveness is our most important contribution to the healing of the world.
—Marianne Williamson, Speaker, Author

You cannot hate other people without hating your self.
—Oprah Winfrey

For the Mother Who Has Everything

My Mother Has Everything So I Wrote Her a Poem

My mother is a multi-faceted jewel
a mirror ball glimmering in an organ music roller rink
She's a child of the forties:
bobby sox and saddle shoes, Frank Sinatra, Frankie Lane,
ring curls and peter pan collars
She's a little sister, big sister, bridesmaid, bride, nurse,
mother, matriarch
She's 70's mom vacuuming to Herrrrrrrrrrrrrrrb Alpert
She's "slap me five, here's your change," the Flip Wilson handshake
in red white and blue pleats
She's bouffant hair, Avon lipstick, black liquid eyeliner, a trail
of Shalimar, and morena good looks to die for
She's a thrusted arm to the solar plexus at red lights
a room temperature washcloth brutalizing your face
a decade of the rosary while careening down the freeway
bedtime prayers and grace before meals.
She's platform shoes and clear plastic heels
Joseph Magnin's, I Magnin's, muzak and mariachi,
Mantovani, Stevie Wonder, Barry Manilow and the Carpenters.
She's wedgie shoes, wedgie hair, scarves and poofy key chains
7-Up in champagne glasses, tea in porcelain cups.
She's the cheerleader that every child and adult needs
xeroxing copies of 3rd grade essays
adorning the house with school kid art
laughing aloud at our silly puns
perennially proud and eternally optimistic.
She's a chismosa but with good intent, never to malign,
only to illuminate.
She is her mother.
She is her sisters.
She's the proud grandmother beginning the cycle anew
so that in the future her grandkids
can write poems like this to her.

—Nancy Marmolejo, poet muse, www.ComadreCoaching.com
For Bunny

Foster Children

I left home when I was six months old. I grew up in many different foster homes. I really didn't have a mother. But there was Mrs. McClellen. I won a baby photo contest at the local department store when I was 4. The name on the award looked different from hers.

I remember how she sat me on her lap in the big chair with brocade fabric and white linen dollies. With tenderness only a real mother can display she explained what it meant to be a foster child. I had other foster mothers but she was the best.

One of the few constants in my childhood was a cigar box. It was made of plain white cardboard with gold trim. It wasn't the box that was valuable, it was the contents.

I used to keep my birthday cards, buttons, and a photo of my real mom. It's where I also kept my ideas and dreams. With all the changes of faces and places, I knew I could always reconnect the threads of my life, just by opening the lid of that little cigar box.

Over the holidays, my wife Janet and I moved into a new house. We love living in St. Petersburg, Florida, where it's always, "Just Another Day in Paradise." Now we keep our stuff in clear plastic boxes, all neatly organized. But I still use a wooden cigar box to keep magazine photos and project ideas for our new dream home.

I don't believe in making New Year's Resolutions, but I think it's a great time to stop and think about what we hope to accomplish this year.

I hope this box helps you capture your ideas, connect with your past, and help you plan for happy and prosperous new years.

—Jerry Gitchel, Speaker, www.MakeTechnologyWork.com

Editor's Note:
Jerry sent his typed contribution to this publication IN an ONYX reserve wooden cigar box!

Four-Legged Children

Mothers of Pets Are Mothers All The Same

When I was divorced a few years ago, my ex-wife got custody of our pet, Jake, an amiable German Shepherd. Jake was a wonderful dog and she loved him as she would a child. And when he died earlier this year, I urged her to get a new dog as quickly as possible and she has done so. To her credit, she adopted Zeta, a true mutt and a Katrina hurricane survivor from the Gulf Coast.

While everyone recognizes that a pet is not a person, it's always safer not to articulate it in front of a pet owner. And much like most dog owners spell out W-A-L-K, lest they be brought a leash and a set of pleading eyes, it is wise to remember that pets have their feelings. Pets are our loved ones, too. For many, are they children they never had and the mother love a woman lavishes on her pet is usually awesome to behold.

When praising mothers, when remembering the gifts they share, a word should be said for Jake and Tigger and Remnant and for all those others who can only chirp, bark, or purr (the list is representative, not inclusive) who are much more, in the end, dependent upon a mother's love and who also want to say, "Thanks, mom."

—John Reddish

Things I Learned about Love from My Cat
1. Always be ready to play.
2. When you are happy to see someone, stretch your arms up to them and ask to be picked up.
3. If the person you love forgets to feed you dinner, don't take it personally.
4. Talk to the one you love, incessantly and constantly.
5. Don't be afraid to ask to be touched.
6. Show your love and adoration by bringing presents.
7. Purr when the person you love is anywhere near you.
8. Encourage the person you love to take naps with you.
9. Always comfort the person you love, regardless of whether they need emotional or physical comfort.
—Unknown

Single Woman, Mother to Cats

It's such a cliche, isn't it? Single woman, mother to cats. But, hey, it's true, at least for me and a bunch of my cat-loving friends. That maternal nature has to come out somewhere, and with animals it's just so easy and natural. Listen to this and tell me if it's not a little bit like being a mom to a human child.

We cat mothers are always going on and on about how clever our "kids" are.

Mother A: "You won't believe this! Pookie figured out how to open the door to the pantry. Pretty amazing for someone with no opposable thumbs."

Mother B: "Hey, that's nothing. Shadow watches TV, and his favorite show is CSI: Miami."

How many times have you seen a cat mom proudly say "Thank you" when you compliment her beautiful kitty, as if she had given birth to it? (I stop just short of keeping cat photos in my wallet.)

Like any single mom, I would never think of getting involved with a man who didn't like my "kids."

Then there is the tendency for us to talk to our cats like they're people. And guess what? They actually understand, and often talk back. Here's a recent conversation I had with Pearlie.
"What do you think you're doing?"
(Look of guileless surprise.) Nothing.
"Don't give me that."
(Beaming and batting eyelashes.)
No, really, I don't know what you mean. Aren't I cute?

"How many times do I have to tell you to stay off the kitchen table!"
(Frowning.) What's the big deal? OK, I can see you're mad, I'm going!

All kidding aside (pardon the pun), I may not have children, but my cats give me a chance to flex those maternal muscles to bask in the love and affection they share with me, to worry and fuss when they're sick, to be amazed by what they understand, to laugh at their playfulness, to cherish their companionship, and to look forward to coming home to them each day.

—Lois Smith

More Than Words

The golden mare lay next to the scruffy foal.
She loves him more than words can say.
Even though he may not be the tallest, cutest or most beautiful.
She loves him for who he is and knows that he has a bright future
She does not know what it may hold
but she will gladly offer her support.
Gazing down upon the foal she gently licks his head
and thinks of the great joy he has brought to her life.

— Shenay Kloss, Age 12 —

CATS & DOGS

Dogs come when they're called; cats take a message
and get back to you later.
—Mary Bly

It is possible to buy love, you can buy a dog!
—Monica Denny, Mother of twin teenage boys

The greatest love is a mother's; then a dog's; then a sweetheart's.
—Polish Proverb

My husband and I are either going to buy a dog or have a child.
We can't decide whether to ruin our carpets or ruin our lives.
—Rita Rudner

Some people own cats and go on to lead normal lives.
—Unknown

It is impossible to keep a straight face in the presence of kittens.
—Cynthia E. Varnado

My little dog - a heartbeat at my feet.
—Edith Wharton

JEWEL'S STORY

Alpacas came into my life in the fall of 2004. These intelligent, gentle, exquisite creatures of the camel family are smaller than llamas and relatively calmer too. Raised for their luxurious fleece, my husband and I started a small herd for our enjoyment and retirement. Alpaca females usually breed yearly, so we eagerly anticipated the birth of our first cria (baby alpaca) in the summer. On that momentous day, when Jewel entered our lives, my heart connection to a "four-legged child" exceeded all my expectations. Thus began my proud "motherly bonding" delights.

This story unfolds from Jewel's perspective.

I was born late in the day... I remember wobbling around the big corral and discovering lots of other four-legged animals besides my Mom. Mommy Julie, who thrilled about the fact that I took my first steps at only 10 minutes old! (I guess it's usually one hour.)

Well since the sun began setting before my white fleece could dry naturally, and it was 48 degrees, Mommy became troubled about me getting cold. By 10pm she finished using her hair dryer and fluffing me up so that I stopped shivering. I remember all the camera flashes from Daddy.

I tried several times to find Mom's milk, but kept coming up dry. It was so dark! Finally Mommy and Daddy helped guide me to the "milk machine," I suckled for five minutes and gulped the rich juices (colostrum that Mommy said I needed to build my immune system) I guess it was a really big deal, because Mommy Julie gave a huge sigh.

As daylight broke I located Mom's milk a lot easier. With every gulp I felt stronger and stronger, and braver and braver. Mommy says that I could be a confident leader since the rest of the herd followed me wherever I went.

Mommy declares that I am way above the average size since I weigh 21 pounds and display lots of energy at 12 hours old.

Well, I'm off to keep exploring this new world.

—As interpreted by Julie Roy, Speaker, Alpaca rancher
www.AlpacasAV.com, www.JulieRoyCoach.com

FUR CHILDREN

I was a shy, quiet child growing up. Although I made friends, I rarely had more than one or two good ones and was perfectly content to spend most of my time alone. Frequently my nose would be buried in a good book, or if it wasn't I was outside playing with some of our many animals (cows, sheep, dog and cat). In Elementary School I had rabbits of my own, and I spent many happy hours talking to them and petting them, even taking them out on "walks" in the pasture so they could get fresh grass.

By late Elementary School I was longing for something larger that could fly me away into the fantasy land I so often visited. Every afternoon for what seemed like years found me in the far far back corner of the pasture standing on Grandfather Wishing Rock. That massive old mossy boulder was where we went to stand, arms and face raised to the heavens, to send forth our deepest desires and longings. What was I wishing for so strongly and intently? A pony. A four-footed friend that I could go explore the world on and with.

And a pony I got. That little shaggy brown pony hauled me all over the yard, then all around the neighborhood, and finally even further afield. We'd race the wind and chase caterpillars and butterflies, jump across logs in the woods, and I even tried for a time to teach him some tricks thinking for sure he was smart enough to be in the circus. Alas, he was smart enough not to learn.

By High School that pony had gone to live with smaller neighbors and I had a full-sized horse to better accommodate my long legs. Taller, faster, stronger, that horse and I could range much further afield. Best of all, my senior year we had her bred and she delivered a foal. I was such a proud mama that I made up and sent out birth announcements.

That was the first time I knew for sure that animals came into my life to help me through the tough times. The transition from High School to the working world and college were not easy years for me. It was always such a relief to escape on horseback into the woods and spend hours just roaming, seeing where we would end up, not having to worry about things. On horseback I felt at peace with the world, and was just blissfully alive and listening, watching, smelling all the miracles that were occurring. Direction in life, career, relationships? I didn't know how to handle them then. Still don't always now.

A few years later, I moved away from home and got married. The horses came with me, but it got more and more difficult to find room for them in my life and finances. And when, in time, my husband got a great job offer from out of state, it was time for us to part. Moving to California meant no more horses and for a few years I was without a fur angel in my life.

Luckily one day a tiny snuggly Dachshund puppy named Trevor came into my life and heart. He has been the joy of my life for the past 10 years, and has helped through some of the rough spots life always brings us. Together we have explored all the parks and forests in the area, met lots of friendly dog-loving people, traveled cross country and back, and had many exciting adventures. He has to be one of the most spoiled little dogs around - he's been hiking and camping, mountain biking, motorcycling, sledding, surfing, and even likes to swing on the swingset. Go figure.

But isn't that what being a parent is all about?
Showing your child the world and what a wondrous exciting place it can be?

"Ever notice, CAT spelled backwards does not spell GOD.
He is your friend, your partner, your defender, your dog.
You are his life, his love, his leader.
He will be yours, faithful and true, to the last beat of his heart.
You owe it to him to be worthy of such devotion."
(Author unknown)

—Dianne Onstad

Science Fiction Feline?

Who says you can't understand the language your pets speak?
My orange, short-hair Tabby, Tigger, is so expressive my neighbors and clients understand what he's saying... and he's not very vocal at all. Just by watching his facial expressions, I can tell when it's his time to go down for his nap. In the morning I tell him, "Time to get up" which he does. In the evening, with a simple "Time for bed" he jumps up on the bed... and when *Stargate SG:1* is on TV, he sits and watches all the Sci-Fi shows with me, munching popcorn at my side!
Series re-runs? You name it: *Star Trek: The Next Generation; Voyager; Deep Space 9;* or *Enterprise;* he's sitting at my side!

—Sheryl Roush

Gardener of Love

Love is like happiness:
* the harder we seek it, the more it eludes us.*
Only when we can give it freely can it come back to us.
                              - Cynthia Brian

When I was young, my mom said something that terrified me. She loved her children so much, she said, that she'd cut off her right arm to save our lives. I had nightmares that she might actually have to do it. Then how would she garden. Worse yet, how could she hug us?

My Mom was a dedicated gardener. Everything she planted grew to be beautiful and bountiful. She spent so much time "pulling hoses" that we always joked that she'd be watering the gardens of heaven. More than anything, Mom planted love. She sacrificed selflessly to give her children great food, a great education, and great self-esteem and self-worth. Because we lived on a farm, she and Dad drove us over a hundred miles a day to school and back. When we forgot our lunches, she'd make another trip to be sure we ate.

Our vegetables came from our own organic gardens, and the fruit was plucked fresh daily from our trees. She taught gardening and healthy cooking techniques to us and other 4-H members.

At Christmas, Dad would take us kids shopping, and we'd each buy Mom our favorite present. (Every Christmas, Mom got five flannel Mother Hubbard nightgowns!) For her birthdays, we showered her with homemade gifts such as cookies, colored leaves, knitted items, and hand-framed photos. We cooked her a special dinner, and Dad always made a big to-do about his "queen." We treasured her dearly within the family, but we'd never celebrated her publicly.

Why is it that Mom's everywhere plan celebrations for everyone, yet rarely are recognized themselves?

At the young age of 63, Mom became a widow. She and my Dad had been madly, deeply, completely in love. His death left her devastated and alone.

When her seventieth birthday approached, my two sisters, my brother, and I decided it was time to give Mom, our gardener of love, a big surprise party to show our appreciation for all those years.

We divided up the duties. Patty's family worked on invitations and catering. Fred arranged for lighting and the cake. Deb and I handled the decor, choosing a garden theme so Mom could take the decorations home afterward. We booked a rural firehouse and started early on a Saturday morning to transform it into a Garden of Eden.

All her children, grandchildren, and spouses came to help set up. Trellises, birdhouses, hoses, water buckets, garden tools, rakes, potted plants, candles, potpourri, garden lights, hummingbird feeders, and all types of beautiful accessories adorned the tables and walls, while hundreds of balloons in wine colors of cabernet, chardonnay, rose, and champagne floated through the air. It was gorgeous. Then the guests started to arrive, hundreds of them, laden with more gardening gifts and bringing their wonderful stories of Mom.

Mom arrived to a fireworks and rocket display, thanks to her grandson Justin, and was totally surprised. The love that filled that firehouse could have ignited a real fire. To have reached the age of seventy and to have so many true friends and loving relatives celebrating her life was indescribably wonderful. As people danced, ate, and laughed, I realized that the only thing in life that truly endures is love.

Love is the deepest of all emotions. Fear and hate are awfully powerful, but love can beat them both. We are shaped and defined by who and what we love. Mom had given love all her life, and this day, her seventieth birthday, others paid tribute and gave love to a loving person.

As Goethe said, "Love is the reward of love."

Sometimes love may seem a rare commodity, but like a garden, it can be nurtured from the harshest soil.

My Mom taught us Seven Rules for a Loving World:

1. Make other people feel good.
2. Make other people look good.
3. Help them meet their needs.

4. Applaud their achievements, no matter how small.
5. Go for win-win solutions.
6. Say "I love you" often and mean it.
7. Expect the best from others.
   People often become what you believe they are.

She would tell us to start somewhere, anywhere.

French poet Antoine de Saint Exupéry has his Little Prince explain, "We see accurately only with our hearts. The essentials are invisible to the eye."

Nearly everyone says they would like more love in their lives. To have love, we must give love. You won't have to cut off your arm to show your love, but you can be like my Mom and plant seeds of happiness and reap a garden of love.

© 2006 Cynthia Brian, Reprinted with permission.

Cynthia Brian, Speaker, Author *Chicken Soup for the Gardener's Soul, Be the Star You Are!*®, and *Miracle Moments*®.
www.BeTheStarYouAre.org
www.star-style.com

GLAD FOR YOU

My mother was an achiever. She lived all of her life in rural South Dakota; however, her rural life did not stop her from wanting to make her mark on the world.

Due to poor crops, mother had to go back to teaching school in a one room school house - she had students in 7 grades working in the same room. At this time, she was also taking care of her three children and doing extensive gardening, especially flower gardening.

There was no garden club in our town, so mother joined a garden club in a neighboring town. Then she formed a club in our town. She became the president of the state garden club. She was not satisfied with presenting and entering flower shows - she had to learn how to be judge the flower shows and even with failing eyesight, she was sought out to judge the flower shows.

Mother, with my Father's help, organized the first ever (and I believe only one ever) **Wonderful World of Glads** - an international flower show of gladiolas via slides.

Mother did not feel that the gardening would leave a lasting memorial, so she took up writing novels regarding the homesteading of the Dakotas as well as writing children stories and poems. She did have three books of poems published; however, her novels were kept for her family to learn and remembers some of the hardships her parents and grandparents experienced.

Although her failing eyesight (legally blind) caused her to give up driving, she continued to live in her apartment and, at 85 years of age, she purchased a word processor to help with her writing as her handwriting became illegible.

Mother instilled in her children the idea that we must keep busy and trying no matter what we chose to do. To stop trying was equivalent to dying mentally.

—Darrell Zeller, son

Generations

This poem was given to me on a sepia toned, well-aged piece of paper with the distinctive crooked type of an antique typewriter. It was composed by my great-grandmother, Anna Green, who has become something of a legend in our family. I feel a kindred spirit to my great grandmother. She was a talented person whose inspiration led her to try many creative things.

With tears in his eyes, my uncle handed this antiquated poem to me after my Grandmother's funeral. "I thought you should have this especially after what you wrote about Gram."

"Gram" was the affectionate term many of us grandchildren used to call my grandmother, and the author of the poem was her mother. I had just delivered my tribute to Gram, my last goodbye, at her funeral the day before. With tears in my eyes, I received the poem feeling as though a torch had been passed from generation to generation. I will always treasure this special poem, and now I feel honored that I can share it with others.

Motherhood, by Anna Green, Circa 1912
At last, I've passed in thro' the gate
That leads into that longed for land.
And only those that pass therein
They alone can understand
What joy, what bliss and happiness
When first you gaze upon the form
That came into your life to bless,
And brought with it all loves charm.
There is no power on earth below,
Like that sent from the heights above,
To forge the links of life into
One golden chain of love.
It matters not what'er ye be
Queen, peasant and all other,
God placed all in equality
When He was choosing Mothers.
And while I'm standing in the land
Where my sisters too have stood
I know God led me by the hand
Thro' the gates of Motherhood.

—Heather Brock
© 2006 Heather Brock Reprinted with permission.

To my wonderful mother on her 65th birthday

How can I ever express to you my deepest gratitude for all of the love, devotion, and support you have showered over me with unending enthusiasm over the past 35 years of my life.

You have given me an incredible gift, the desire to life to its fullest. Your optimism and zest for life has filled me with a passion to do more, to be the best I can be, and to pursue all of my dreams.
Now that I am a mother myself, I can truly appreciate the incredible journey you experienced to raise five, healthy and happy children.

Mom, you have always been the cheerleader by my side. You have always greeted me with a warm hug and a smile, and you have always supported me with unconditional love. When I am feeling ill, I can always expect a pone call with words of true concern and empathy. To this day, I still find notes and cards that you sent to me over the years with words of support and encouragement and always full of pride. How can I forget how much I looked forward to your letters with warm news from home and happy thoughts while away at summer camps as a child?

How can I forget the excitement of using the same speech that you wrote with your father in high school when running for Class President, that helped bring me to the same victory in my high school, 30 years later?

How can I forget the thrill of opening all of the special gifts you gave me for my daughter to be, and watching the sparkle in your eye to see your own daughter entering the wonderful world of motherhood?
And how can I forget the first time you held my daughter, with the same love, gentleness, and warmth you always showered over me?

May your legacy be carried from generation to generation.

With love and gratitude,
—Francine Geller, "Franny," twin sister to Amy, married, 3 children
In tribute to Sandra Schrift, Mother

Gift from My Son

A UNIQUE GIFT OF LIFE FROM MY SON

Considerably late in life, I gave birth to my son. I was enjoying being a busy being new Mom, breast-feeding and basking in the glory of my little miracle. Fortunately, my pregnancy was fairly easy and I had a very healthy baby, 7lbs. 8 oz, 21 and a half inches long, in spite of my age! My doctor had advised that when I stopped breast-feeding to allow a little time and we'd then schedule a mammogram. There was no urgency, just advice.

While I was still nursing, the very tip of my nipple developed a very small sore. I had had some difficulty nursing and some related irritations; and this small sore seemed no more than part of that. When I first pointed it out to my doctor, she said it was nothing. She thought it was a breast-feeding irritation and would soon go away. I stopped breast-feeding and gave my nipple time to heal. It didn't. Conscious that my body didn't usually take this long to heal, I went in to see another doctor, get a second opinion, and scheduled a mammogram. Immediately following the mammogram was a consult with the surgeon. He diagnosed me with a rare breast cancer that affects men as well as women called DCIS and Paget's Disease. My dismay and shock made it hard for me to find my way out of the doctor's office! As I sat in my car in the hospital parking garage, I screamed and screamed, wondering if I would live long enough to raise my now two-year-old son.

After the initial shock, there were moments when I would feel a tremendous calm in spite of all the emotional chaos. When I could be in touch with my feelings, I knew that God was with me through this entire ordeal. Two weeks after diagnosis, and just two weeks before Christmas, I had a single mastectomy! On Christmas Eve, my gift was the removal of the surgical drainage tubes. I went through chemotherapy treatment and lost 95% of my hair. Although I never went completely bald, wigs and hats became my new fashion statement. I loved that I could put my head out of the car window not mess up my hair!

Every woman's experience with cancer is very personal and no two people seem to have the exact same experience even though we all go through similar treatments. One thing that was amazing to me is people that you barely know will step up and lend their help and support in unexpected and amazing ways. And sometimes, people whom you would expect to be supportive are not. Many times close friends and family are at a total loss as what to do to help their loved one. They are so afraid for you and for themselves.

I came to realize that although having Cancer is an awful experience, God meant for me to go through it for some reason. It is also not the worst challenge a person can have. I can look at the challenges that others go through and feel I am blessed that mine was "only" breast cancer. There is always something worse.

The attitude you chose to have in a crisis is also of major importance to the success of the outcome. No, it's not easy. But find what is important to you and focus on that. For me, it was living to raise my son for a long, long time to come. We may not understand what God wants from us, but we can have trust and just go with it as best we can.

No matter what we go through and the challenges we face, there are sweet spots. Don't get me wrong; it doesn't take the tragedy out of the experience. But when we look for even the smallest, tiniest glimmer of what is positive out of the experience we can and will have a new perspective. These are our unique and unexpected gifts.

When I asked my Aunt Mary, who had gone through breast cancer twice, with two mastectomies years apart, "How did this experience change you?" What she shared with me is what I have since heard many other women say in similar ways, "You quit sweating the small stuff. I learned to appreciate my children and husband even more. Every day is precious." Like Aunt Mary, I smile now when my son does something that might have previously made me angry. In the grand scheme of things, it doesn't really matter. I am thankful to be here for him and he for me. He is the most precious thing in the world to me.

After the mastectomy, in my rare case of sick-sense-of-humor, I wondered, "If I had had a double mastectomy would that mean I could take my shirt off in the summer, like a boy, and no one would care?" Yes, well many would care, but it was a rather funny thought just the same!

More and more women can—and do survive breast cancer. If you find anything unusual for your own body and how it would normally react, get it checked! Don't ignore those little things that just don't seem quite right. Many of the wome whom have lost their lives to breast cancer often ignored their early warning signs.

According to the American Cancer Society, one out of seven women will be diagnosed with breast cancer.

If you have a loved one diagnosed with cancer, you will find a free article available o my website, "How To Help Her With Cancer," with dozens of little ideas and suggestions on how you can help your loved one through this difficult time. Friends and family are invaluable to the healing process.

Throughout my ordeal, I choose to have courage, faith and persistence. I trust if you should find yourself in a similar situation, you will find the strength to do the same.

With love and blessings to you.

Eln

—Eln Albert, Speaker, Author of *The Magic of Moms*
A leading expert in how people interact, react and influence each other and motherly qualities working women bring to the workplace. www.ElnAlbert.com.

God

Love is the face of God.
—Amma (Mother), Mata Amritanandamayi, India
Messages from Amma: In the Language of the Heart, www.amma.org

People see God every day, they just don't recognize him.
—Pearl Bailey

When I stand before God at the end of my life,
I would hope that I would not have a single bit of talent left,
and could say, "I used everything you gave me."
—Erma Bombeck

Every evening I turn my worries over to God.
He's going to be up all night anyway.
—Mary C. Crowley

See God in every person, place, and thing, and all will be well in
your world.
—Louise L. Hay

I have never met a person whose greatest need was anything other
than real, unconditional love. You can find it in a simple act of
kindness toward someone who needs help. There is no mistaking
love. You feel it in your heart. It is the common fiber of life, the flame
that heals our soul, energizes our spirit and supplies passion to our
lives. It is our connection to God and to each other.
—Elizabeth Kubler-Ross

Be willing to believe in a greater way about yourself.
Let your heart be receptive to God's Spirit and guidance.
Have the courage to make the decision to allow the possibility of
greatness in you. Take risks beyond your boundaries,
and God is right there with you.
—Mary Manin Morrissey, Author *Life Keys*

I know God will not give me anything I can't handle.
I just wish that He didn't trust me so much.
—Mother Teresa

What you are is God's gift to you.
What you become is your gift to God.
—Eleanor Roosevelt

You can tell the size of your God by looking at the size of your worry
list. The longer your list, the smaller your God.
—Unknown

The God that gives us life gives us the tools for our expansion
and is not responsible for how we use those tools.
—Joni Wilson, Voice Expert, Author *Thunder Behind the Silence:
When a Woman Finds Her Voice,* www.JoniWilsonVoice.com

Is God a Man or a Woman?
The answer to the question is Neither—God is ***That***.
But if you must give God a gender, God is more female than male,
for HE is contained in SHE.

That infinite power is God, and there is only one.
Christians call God *Christ*;
Muslims call God *Allah*;
Hindus call God *Shiva, Krishna, Mother*—but *all* are the same God.

There is only one God.
The supreme Self says, "However you conceive of me, I am there."

All over the world Mother (Divine Love, Motherhood, God/Goddess)
hears her children's heart calling.
She longs to soothe their painful yearnings and lead them to
eternal Light. Mother does not distinguish among nations, for
She is everywhere–all people are her darling children.
There are many petals on a flower but the flower is one–
the world is a flower and every nation a petal.
To Mother, all are One.

Life and God are One.

—Amma (Mother), Mata Amritanandamayi, India
Messages from Amma: In the Language of the Heart, www.amma.org

WHY GOD CREATED CHILDREN

Whenever your children are out of control, you can take comfort from the thought that even God's omnipotence did not extend to His own children. After creating heaven and earth, God created Adam and Eve.
And the first thing he said was "DON'T!"
"Don't what?" Adam replied.

"Don't eat the forbidden fruit," God said.

"Forbidden fruit? We have forbidden fruit?
Hey Eve..we have forbidden fruit!"
"No Way!"
"Way!"
"Do NOT eat the fruit!" said God.
"Why?"
"Because I am your Father and I said so!" God replied, wondering why He hadn't stopped creation after making the elephants.

A few minutes later, God saw His children having an apple break and He was ticked! "Didn't I tell you not to eat the fruit?" God asked.
"Uh huh," Adam replied.
"Then why did you?"said the Father.
"I don't know," said Eve.
"She started it!" exclaimed Adam.
"Did not!"
"Did too!"
"DID NOT!"

Having had it with the two of them, God's punishment was that Adam and Eve should have children of their own.
Thus the pattern was set and it has never changed.

BUT THERE IS REASSURANCE IN THE STORY!
If you have persistently and lovingly tried to give children wisdom and they haven't taken it, don't be hard on yourself.

If God had trouble raising children, what makes you think it would be a piece of cake for you?

—Unknown

Grandmothers

Grandmothers are the people who take delight in hearing babies breathing on the telephone.

Grandmothers are moms with lots of frosting.

Grandmothers are just "antique" little girls.

Grandmothers hold our tiny hands for just a little while, but our Hearts forever.

A grandmother is a babysitter who watches the kids instead of the TV

A grandparent is old on the outside but young on the inside.

GIFTS FROM GRANDMOTHER

In May of 2002, I received my Bachelors Degree. This ceremony was put into motion seventy years ago. My grandmother had earned a scholarship for college. Societal norms dictated that she relinquish it. Few women of color attended college in the 1930s. My mother's generation continued the dream of higher action. Financial difficulties and having children slowed the process. The love and wisdom of two generations of women laid the foundation for my degree. I was the first female in the family to receive a Bachelors. I am thankful for their shoulders that I climbed upon to reach this goal. From the smiles on their faces, it was clear that we all graduated that day.
—Renee Carter, Speaker

WHAT ARE GRANDMAS FOR?
Grandmas are for stories about things of long ago.
Grandmas are for caring about all the things you know.
Grandmas are for rocking you and singing you to sleep.
Grandmas are for giving you nice memories to keep.
Grandmas are for knowing all the things you're dreaming of.
But, most of all, Grandmas are for love.

—Unknown

WHAT IS A GRANDMA?

A grandma is warm hugs and sweet memories.
She remembers all of your accomplishments
and forgets all of your mistakes.
She is someone you can tell your secrets and worries to,
And she hopes and prays that all your dreams come true.
She always loves you, no matter what.
She can see past temper tantrums and bad moods,
And makes it clear that they don't affect how precious you are to her.
She is an encouraging word and a tender touch.
She is full of proud smiles.
She is the one person in the world who loves you with all her heart,
Who remembers the child you were
and cherishes the person you've become.
—Barbara Cage—

Grandparents bestow upon their grandchildren
The strength and wisdom that time
And experience have given them.
Grandchildren bless their Grandparents
With a youthful vitality and innocence
That help them stay young at heart forever.
Together they create a chain of love
Linking the past with the future.
The chain may lengthen,
But it will never part...
— Unknown —

Ever since the day I was born.
You have nurtured me with love and kindness.
You have been someone I can believe in,
And someone I can depend upon.
In this world I am just starting to understand.
And it's important to me that you know
How grateful that I am,
For all that you give to me,
For all that you teach me,
And for the strength I will always have,
Because of you, grandma.
— Unknown —

MY FIRST GRANDCHILD

When I picked up Jackie she smiled
a crooked toothless grin.
She made great yawn,
And I melted.
Holding close the black fuzzy haired
Facsimile of her mother,
I knew that nothing would ever
Be the same again.
That loving cannot be told in words,
It just flows back and forth,
Between us... never stopping,
Like the tide.
This is my first grandchild,
She's the pride of my life,
And the joy of my world.
A truly exceptional baby.

MY SECOND GRANDCHILD

Our Dayna is something like a rash,
That tickles where you cannot scratch.
She turned somersaults on the floor,
But smashed into the kitchen door.
She has a certain brand of kisses,
Sticky and wet and so delicious,
That thoughts of discipline turn to ashes,
When blue eyes peek through long black lashes.
Pretending is her favorite game.
A bunny, a kitten - never the same.
Angel, puppy, a bird in flight,
A chicken, a dancer, big red kite.
She entered life in second place.
Yet fills for me a special space.
Like moon and stars or sunny day
She lights my life in every way.

—Rosalie Ferrer Kramer, Speaker, Poet, Author—
www.authorsden.com/rosaliefkramer

ROSIE SWEET ROSIE

So many stories she was willing to share,
This kind, sweet lady with the silver gray hair.
One hundred five years she lived with such grace,
Through troubled times many hardships she faced.

I've had a good life I've heard her say,
When it's my time Jesus come take me away.
She has given to many so much for so long,
Our lives will be changed now that Rosie is gone.

Loved by all whose lives she touched,
This gentle sweet lady was loved so much.
God blessed us all with her in our lives,
Rosie, sweet Rosie, so caring and wise.

She blessed our lives with grace and love,
We thank our Father in Heaven above.
Rosie, sweet Rosie, so precious and kind,
A sweeter person we will never find.

We love her so and she'll always be dear,
In memories she gave us that we can hold near.
Our lives will be different now that Rosie is gone,
But we'll see her in Heaven before too long.

The time is here and we must part,
Rosie, sweet Rosie, you live in our hearts!

— Judith A. Duran —

Written about Rosie Helton
a wonderful grandmother-in-law

DEAR LORD

Dear Lord if I have to be this way,
Please take me now I cannot stay.
I can't recall what I said yesterday,
I dread repeating it anyway.

And don't let me stay so long a while,
That I have to fake another smile,
When the packer in the grocery store,
Inquires if I need his help once more

Alas that phone's ringing off the hook.
My granddaughter says she's learning to cook,
And that her first baby is on the way,
So please Dear Lord don't take me TODAY!

Now I want to stay on my sojourn,
Until my new great-grandchild is born.
And maybe until there'll be another,
Who can also call me great-grandmother

Old age isn't perfect but it's never a bore,
'Specially with new little ones to adore.
And so, Dear Lord, I pray you'll ignore
All that dumb stuff I told you before.

—Rosalie Ferrer Kramer, Speaker, Poet
Author *Senior Humor*
www.authorsden.com/rosaliefkramer

Tribute to Gram
In loving memory of Helen V. Anderson, 12/31/1916 - 12/11/2005

As read at her funeral services on 12/17/2005

It's an interesting thing when one lives a full life. We, younger, see her as always . . .well, old. Was Grandma always a Grandma? No. She was once just a woman and before that a young girl who once was a babe that gurgled and giggled and cooed. As her mother cradled her and nestled her to her chest she prayed God's blessing and protection over her little new life. She was her papa's pride and her mama's joy. No doubt she was poked and kissed and squeezed by her big sisters as she scooted and crawled and took her first shaky steps. She was, after all, once just a baby.

As a young girl, I'm sure she skipped and hopped and scraped her knee. She twirled and danced as her papa played the fiddle. She teased the boys and giggled with her girlfriends who shared little girl secrets. She sat in a solemn, quiet church trying to suppress her laughter until it bubbled out when she could hold it no more. She got stern looks and reprimands and still went off to create another fun adventure. Perhaps, she scrunched her nose and furrowed her brow and refused to eat her spinach or turnips or broccoli. Because once she WAS a young girl.

On her porch one day in a crisp cotton dress, a handsome neighbor boy caught her eye in a way they had never gazed before. She felt butterflies and love's anxiety. She was courted and wooed. She heard sweet whispers of fresh new love, and soon she became a young bride. She had dreams and hopes of her life with her love. A new home? Babies? What could the future bring?

She was once a new mother and I can only guess that she delighted in feeling the first flutters and kicks. She talked to her sisters about what to expect. When she nursed and cradled her own baby girl, perhaps she prayed the same prayer her own mother prayed as she kissed her daughter's tender head, "God, bless and protect her life for all her days when I'm near and far, when I'm here and when I'm gone. God keep her well and keep her safe lest my whole heart should break."

Can you imagine a time when she softly, tenderly brushed a little curl from her daughter's eye, and then held her cheek -the perfect fit-in the palm of her adoring hand? Or dressing her boys in their crisp little suits and carefully tying the laces as they wiggled and squirmed? Straightening a tie and giving an approving wink.?

Or gently wiping away dirty tears with the hem of her shirt after a particularly hard scuff.

Can you imagine how her heart broke once, twice, and then again as she watched her children struggle? How she must have plead "Please God, let me. Let me struggle. Let me hurt. Let me fight. Let me fever. Take their pain and give it all to me. Just let their precious lives be free." She did. Because she was once a mom.

She was a business owner. Before the books and guides and the groups for support, she balanced, she managed her home, her kids, her husband, her friends, her church and her clients.

And so being a woman, she comforted a disheartened friend and prayed God's peace for her life. She cried herself to sleep I'm sure more than once. She squealed with joy and contorted her face with uncontrollable laughter at something unexpectedly funny.

One day, her kids happy now with spouses, grown and gone, she enjoys another new phase–"Grandma." Giggling again, reading, singing and telling stories to her grandkids. In the middle of her joy, she faced the chance she would have to begin again and raise four of her young grandchildren... alone. Another prayer "God bless them and protect them an ocean away. They are so far . . ."

But even though she was a baby, a girl, a young woman, a bride, and a mom, to me she'll always just be... Grandma.

This Grandma who read Bible stories, made up jokes just to make us laugh, sang church songs to us in nearly baritone. She cuddled us the way every great grandma should. She told us the things a loving grandma would. She told us stories of God and family legends. She prayed. She prayed, and she prayed.

What exactly is heaven? I don't exactly know. But I believe there is perfect clarity, perfect peace, perfect love and she is there with her perfect Savior as the baby, the girl, the young woman, the bride, the mom, and the Grandma who is also known as–"Great!"

—Heather Brock
© 2006 Heather Brock   Reprinted with permission.

LET ME TELL YOU ABOUT MY GRANDMOTHER!

I have learned many things on how to care for little kids such as babies from you. I learned things to keep them busy and feeding them. I also love coming to your house because you have a variety of cool clothes, shoes, canes, belly dancing stuff, and jewelry. It was always fun to dress up and then come out and act out a skit that you make up on the spot directed around what we were wearing. I brought a friend a couple years ago to your house with us. She still to this day says, "Brittney when can I come back to your grandma's house? It was soooo fun to dress up and act out stuff! She has cool clothes and things. You have a REALLY COOL AND FUN GRANDMA!!!!"

—Brittney Schrift, Age 12, grand daughter of Sandra Schrift

MOTHER OF 6

My grandmother, Nellie Reimers Lundquist, was just under five foot tall, condensed power and fortitude unmatched in anyone I'd ever seen. I still clearly remember her fortitude, perseverance and great sense of humor. She always had fresh homemade cookies in the pantry, anticipating our visit, and wanting to have time with us, out of the kitchen. She raised seven kids, twenty-two grandkids, and hundreds of great-grandkids! A daughter, and wife of a rancher, she had hands of steel, a body built for severe winters, yet a heart that would melt for a grand-daughters plea... All the kids were visiting the Iowa farm over vacation, and helping out with the chores of running 100+ acres. My parents and brothers were bailing hay that day. I was too young to help at six years old. A small rabbit had been pinned in the bailing wire, and would surely die trapped without food. I heard about it and begged to keep it. Grandma was very clear about her dislike for rabbits due to that they ate up all her fresh vegetables in her beloved garden. She gave in... and for that summer, I was the proud mother of "Bugs," feeding it, nurturing it back to health.

—Sheryl Roush, one of 22 Nellie's grandkids

FINAL WORDS OF TRIBUTE

The last thing my brother in law said to my mother was
"Go get your Crown, granny, you deserve it."
—Morgie Peirano

Guilt & Motherhood

Guilt and Motherhood: They go hand in hand

Guilt seems to be the common denominator which spans all cultures, ages, marital status, and economic backgrounds. We can all agree that guilt tends to impact our daily lives including the way we parent and our view of ourselves. Basically, there is not enough of you to go around, which leaves you feeling guilty because you are unable to fulfill the needs of those around you.

Guilt can be compounded by various factors. Our age can be a leading cause of guilt. Either we are not old enough or "too old" to parent. We are parenting at all ages, these days. Guilt makes us second-guess ourselves. "I do not know as much or I cannot provide enough as other mothers." Or my favorite, "I am not a good mother, because..." For the "younger" mothers, we tend to second-guess our abilities to parent due to our "inexperience" or lack of resources. For the "mature" mothers, we tend to second-guess our abilities to parent due to our "exhaustion" or inner fears. In both cases, we tend to compare ourselves to other mothers and decide that "they" must be doing EVERYTHING better than we are.

The truth is (or at least my truth) parenting is difficult for all, no matter what age, economic background or ethnicity. Being a single parent is truly a difficult job; one has the common guilt associated with parenthood which then is multiplied with the added guilt of being a single parent. One never feels that he/she is providing enough for his/her children. And the truth is, parenting is a team effort and when all of the responsibility is placed on one person, needs can go unmet. However, one person can only do as much as one person can do. That is just a fact. Understanding limitations is the first step to accepting the reality that we are doing the best we can.

Our goal is to be a "Good Enough Mother." This is the acceptance that yes, some needs are going to go unmet and the child may have to make some sacrifices BUT Good Enough is Enough! Children will grow and develop into successful adults even when (or especially when) all their needs were not met. This allows for children to learn skills to achieve their own needs.

We can put an inordinate amount of pressure on ourselves to be able to do everything. Women do have superpowers, but we all have our limits. There will be times when our kids act out in public, have a temper tantrum at the grandparents' house or throw a fit in the grocery store and these behaviors do not reflect our parenting abilities. However, it is difficult in the moment not take these behaviors personally, fearing that some how we caused it by not being "good enough." Other people's children don't have temper tantrums, right?

I enjoy leading parenting groups because this setting provides parents the opportunity to hear that temper tantrums happens in every family, and that even when we are doing our very best, we still may feel guilty about our role as a parent, wife or friend. I describe the developmental stages o parenthood. Briefly, when children are young and dependent on us to meet their every need (or at least their basic needs) or guilt levels are high.

This can last through pre-school and even into elementary school. But, as our children grow and become more independent, we can get a break from our guilt. Fortunately, there is a period where we can enjoy the benefits of our hard work. For a number of years in elementary school our parenting guilt changes and lessens. We may feel extra pressure and stress from homework and extra curricular activities, but we tend to be a little easier on ourselves.

Often there is a break from our guilt as our children become more independent.

I highlight the role of guilt in our lives in hopes to normalizing these feelings; I believe guilt is universal. From this understanding, we can begin to give ourselves permission to be human, accept our limitations and acknowledge our strengths. Talking to others is good medicine. We understand that we are not alone with these feelings and that it will be o.k. Remember you do have super powers, but you are also human. Be good to yourself and enjoy the guilt free moments. You are "Good Enough!"

—Cindy Hill-Ford, LMFT is a Psychotherapist in private practice. She specializes in adoption and facilitates pre & post adoptive parent support groups and a group for adoptees. Cindy also contracts as a Behavior Specialist for a local foster family agency. www.Adoption-Associates.com

Reprinted with permission.

Headstrong Love

It's truly powerful to look back and re-live all the love. To feel all the love again. My brother Clay and I are blessed to have been raised by a mother so giving of her love. Number seven of eight children, our Mom was born to headstrong French Canadians who schooled all their daughters through Catholic boarding schools in Canada. Yes, the ones run by nuns equipped with "measuring tools."

Her mom, our Mémère, was so headstrong that when our Pépère (our grandfather) told her that he was going to have to relocate the clothesline from where it was attached to their house because of a developing orange tree. Memere responded by swiftly waddling her aging 87-year-old body over to the tree, bent down bedside the tree, and from its base, bent the tree to the ground. I was 12 at the time, and couldn't believe my eyes. I was just glad she didn't make me arm wrestle. And oh-by- the-way, it was the orange tree that was relocated - not the clothesline.

Our Mother was headstrong in her love of her two boys.

Our Mother was diagnosed with Breast Cancer in 1978. I was six. Clay was eight. I still remember the day like it was yesterday. I was sitting on the kitchen table, and Clay was sitting on a chair next to me. Time stood still as my parents tried to explain the situation, that our mother had a serious medical issue that required she undergo surgery immediately. Despite the urgency of the circumstances, it was apparent my Mom's biggest concern was not over her health, but rather how her two boys would handle the situation. Much to her doctor's chagrin, to assuage and comfort us, she postponed her necessary surgery a few days to watch Clay play the part of Peter Rabbit in the middle school Easter play - a part that he had been working so hard on and felt so proud about. I still find it hard to believe, but she's quick to say, "I wouldn't have missed it for the world." Then she beat the cancer. I'm pretty confident that she didn't beat the cancer for herself, she beat it for us. Truly headstrong love. Today, our mother now fights to conquer yet another cancer as she was diagnosed with endometrial cancer in 2002. We are confident she will win this battle!

Clay and I both grew up playing sports. Baseball, basketball, soccer, football, track, cross country, lacrosse... you name it. The combined seasons ran all year long, year in and year out, from the days of tee-ball through our days at Minnechaug Regional High School. The ONLY time our Mom wasn't at one of our games, was when our events coincided, and during those times, more often than not, she somehow managed to catch a portion of each game. "Go Bryce! You can do it!" Not just vocally, I could always feel her presence, and her constant support and belief in us. It wasn't about winning or losing, although I would consider Clay and I are both competitive, it was about supporting us and believing in us to give it our best. That love and support greatly impacted who we are today.

To this day, whenever we're together, we still practice a ritual that has been in existence since the day I can remember. Whenever we leave each other's company, whether it be leaving for work or just to make a quick trip to the grocery store for milk, we give each other a kiss, and say I love you. She always said you never know, and regardless of what happens, she wanted us to know that she loved us. She was a stickler about this. And now, not only do we do it with our Mom, Clay and I do it with our wives.

Mom - On behalf of Clay and I, we thank you for your headstrong love, and for the sacrifices you made in the honor of motherhood. You ALWAYS put your two sons and our family first. We both aspire to be as wonderful of Fathers as you are a Mother to us today and have been throughout our lifetime!

With much love,
Bryce

—Bryce Whiting

Heart of a Soldier's Mother

I knew that if I were to survive missing my 19-year old son while he left for war, the only way I could do it was by asking for support... asking for prayers. Not something I had ever asked for before in a grandiose way. I was the typical overextended mothering type, doing more for others before paying any attention to me and my needs.

And never would I think to reveal anything so private about me– an equally grandiose... heartache.

For the first time, I poured out my heart to family, friends, business associates and even acquaintances... and asked for help.

==

Sent: Thursday, March 03, 2005 9:12 PM
Our hearts are heavy...
... After Michael, my husband, with our daughter, Nicole, tearfully gave our farewells among a smothering of hugs to our son, Dominic. As I write this, he is probably on the plane to Kuwait, where his unit will wait for a few days for the remainder of the battalion, then helo out to Camp Fallujah in Iraq.

I know statistically the percentage of war fatalities is not much different than the statistical percentage of fatalities from car accidents, crime, etc., in the U.S.

I know that the media focuses on the fatalities.

I know Dominic is under God's protection and care and under the powerful prayer support of so many.

I 'know' the likelihood that he will return to us 'just fine.'

Yet as mother of my only son and youngest child, and speaking for Michael and Nicole, our hearts still hurt to send him off to a war zone.

Maybe it hurts so much because we know too well about the realities of war from Michael who served as a medic in Vietnam.

As a mother, I've put off 'feeling' about this. It all finally 'hit me' after the Marines suddenly moved up their deployment a week and shortened their liberty from an expected 3 or 4 days, to only 12 hours.

Dominic clearly wanted to be in the military since he was 5 years old. His father and 2 grandfathers set the precedence with commendable service careers. What is a mother to do?

We ask for your (continued) prayer support for him, his battalion, and the troops that serve. For their safe return. For peace. We thank all who have already given love and support.

My 'work' is cut out for me as I stay busy to help keep my mind positive about all this... I will write again soon.

In the meantime, peace be with you and yours. May you take an extra moment today to look at your children and loved ones with grateful loving eyes and hold them warm and close to you.

Maria
==
I couldn't believe the response! I wrote back with:

Well you touched our hearts! Thank you so very much for your love and prayer support.

And thank you for your patience in responding to you. We were overwhelmed with the responses-emotionally, most definitely yes, and also in number and size. We received almost 200 email responses, which filled 52 pages! I just finished compiling the responses and I'm sending them off by regular mail to Dominic today. I believe he will be overwhelmed as well.

Thank you from the bottom of our hearts. I reached out and you responded with your heart. As the responses came pouring in (many calls, too), I sat and cried as I read them... Many wrote about:
- Also being a parent, relative or friend of someone also in Iraq and relating to the emotion of that
- Of appreciating my sharing a very personal and deep part of me and being moved by my writing
- Of being part of Dominic's 'virtual support team'
- Of gratitude for the military and the sacrifices...
- Of God and the angels protecting...
- Of love and prayers and prayer lists for Dominic, our family, and the entire situation overseas.

I don't know any other way to thank you but to say I love you.
We love you.

I/we do feel much better knowing how Dominic is wrapped in your love and prayers.

With Love, Maria, Michael and Nicole

==
The following eight months took its toll on me... crying to sleep at night, weight gain... keeping myself extremely busy... examining my life: "Had I been the best mother I could be?" etc... All the while we anxiously waited for any news from Dominic... and the day he would come home.

I was so afraid to reveal my tender heart and ask for support...
to cope with a soldier's mother's greatest fears...

I forgot to look at the other side until the time was upon us:
To celebrate this soldier's mother's answered prayers...
==
Sent: Saturday, October 15, 2005 5:18 AM
Subject: Dominic is HOME!

Dominic just arrived–he's home, in our arms, safe and sound!...
==
The prayers protected Dominic's unit of about 250 Marines.
They suffered only one accidental injury on the deployment,
despite being surrounded by fatalities in other units in their same areas during the same time.

I dedicate this story to other mothers of soldiers, with loving prayers to embrace and protect their own and their family's tender hearts, their sons and daughters and their units, and most importantly for all the world...Peace.

© 2006 Maria Carter, www.fallinlovewithyourlife.com

Holidays

My Pretty Santa

They say that Santa's jolly, and has a long white beard;
They say he wears a red suit, and brings gifts every year.

But now that I am older, and see things much more clear,
I'll tell you all a secret, if you will all draw near.

My Santa is so pretty, so loving and so dear;
She'll stay up half the night, to see us smile from ear to ear.

When others are too busy, or simply are not there;
She'll bake and shop and wrap just right, to bring us Christmas cheer.

She knows just what we want, her goal is very clear,
Her loving hands work tirelessly to make Christmas magically appear.

With her lonely, thankless task complete, candy; dolls;
toys and miscellaneous gear;
Bright and early Christmas morn,"Santa came" is all we hear.

And I'll be ever grateful, my wish for her sincere;
God Bless my Santa-Mom, as she has blessed us through the years!

— Rita Lanell Shaw De Los Reyes —
Age 13 at time of writing

Editor's Note:
Today Rita is a mother of three, and grandmother of six

When my daughter was little, she asked
"Is there really a Santa Clause?"
I replied, "What would Christmas be like without a Santa Clause?"
She is now 31 years old, and still believes in Santa.

—Shirlie Cunningham

"FAMILY CIRCUS" CHRISTMAS
Mommy throws a Tantrum!

When I started this vocation called Mother I had it all down. I just knew my children (2, maybe 3) would be the most perfect in the neighborhood. I was going to give June Cleaver a run for her money!! Donna Reed....Ha!!! Betty Crocker, oh pleazzzze!! Over and over again in my head I said Ha!!! Then I actually had a child. And another. And another. And another. And another... boy, this wasn't how I played it all out in my head!!!! Five babies in six years!! Wow!!! Just getting out of the house I had to find shoes to go with 50 little toes... oh, and the socks needed for those same 50 little piggies!! It was and still is an adventure!!

Christmas was a fun time at our house but a frustrating time for me personally. I just could not figure out why I could not have the sit down dinner with everyone pressed, styled, combed, clean, smiling, happy and oh so grateful, singing *Silent Night* in perfect pitch just before the "Norman Rockwell" Christmas dinner was served!!

One particular Christmas I was so frustrated that this was not happening. I tried all the "right" things and when that failed I resorted to bribery, blame, lavish promises and finally at whit's end... a tantrum. Yep. Not just whine, shed a tear then go about life tantrum... a full blown on-my-face-tantrum in the living room in front of the Christmas tree on the floor kicking my feet, pounding my fist, screaming... "Why??! Why?? Why?? and then to have my oldest (who was all of 5 years old), come tell me "Z, Mommy. 'Z' comes after 'Y.' Don't be sad we will work on your alphabet together!! You can get it!!!"

Thank God he didn't know the real reason for my tantrum!!! I dried my tears and looked at them. Really looked at them. They were happy, perplexed at mommy at that moment, but they had all their little hearts needed. A mommy and daddy who loved them. A safe place to put their blankie and to them, a fun place to be. They had more live in playmates than anyone they knew!!!.

I suddenly realized what the problem was. Not the kids–not my husband–but me! Not the me me–but the attitude me.

I missed out of the real wonders of the first few Christmases because of my terrible choice of holiday comfort friends. Yep, the trio Shoulda, Coulda and Woulda and their cousins Only and If had come to once again to the Hall house to "celebrate" the year! I don't remember consciously inviting five more to our already full house... but nonetheless they showed up every year and seemed to be staying longer and longer!! Uninvited... how rude!!!

NO wonder I was so frustrated!!! I kept striving for the "Norman Rockwell" Christmas and kept getting "Family Circus" instead!!! I had my holiday comfort friends cheering me on, again. That year I gave them the boot!!! And I discovered "Family Circus" isn't so bad!!

The Friends still try to visit occasionally, usually when my spirits a bit down... but there is no room!!! I still hold on to the fantasy of "Norman Rockwell" Christmas Dinner but only in my dreams. As I watch my pieces of Heaven laugh, run, play, enjoy each other... I really have made best friends with the "Family Circus." And I learned the whole alphabet too!!

—Terri L. Hall

Contributor's request:
Please do not use any part of this out of context.

Editor's note:
In our conversation receiving permission to print this original work for the first time, Terri added:
"In time God blessed me with a new life (in more ways than one) and now am remarried (for almost 10 years) and have a total of 12 children and 6 grandchildren with one on the way (only 7 kids are still at home). It has been an adventure!!!

I Never Knew My Mother

I never knew my mother.

It's not that I never really knew her, or that we were estranged.
She really wasn't around.

I remember faintly, or at least I remember, down in my cells, her
touch, her voice, her smell. Others will, of course, tell me (time and
time again) that I must be imagining things, that I couldn't possibly
remember anything about her. I don't know why not.

Often times when I am with loving friends and someone brushes
against my shoulder just so, with the lightest of feathery touches,
my mind awakens to another hand, rubbing my cheek ever so softly.
It's such a soft touch. Sometimes when I am out walking in the
breeze and a leaf flutters by the same feelings will well up inside me,
almost as if a warm, loving breath has embraced me. And I always
feel safe. And warm. A soft warmth that spreads from my head to my
toes. I love that I always feel safe when that happens. And in that
moment, I feel the almost imperceptible touch just brush my cheek
and the sense of tremendous surrender. And with that comes the
complete and utter knowledge that I am loved. I know that I can close
my eyes and relax my vigilance and just be.

Sometimes there is a hint of an aroma. It's vaguely floral, with a hint
of baby powder, and something almost like the best smells of a spring
day (just after the spring showers). It's there, and then it's gone, and
yet, it's always with me.

I cannot imagine any memories more firmly embedded than the one
who loves and nurtures, the hand that soothes, cares for, loves,
cherishes, and touches just to be close. It's a primal connection,
mother and daughter.

Now you may say that with all children, in the first days, weeks, and
months, it is a complete bonding. Yes, it is the tactile language of
selfless love shared between a mother and child, yet with a girl, it is
more. For we are alike, mother and daughter, so alike in the woven
fabric of our lives, woven from the same cloth. With a small touch,
the ring of a laugh, the quiet cooing of affections that issue from
mother to daughter, the daughter is welcomed into the loving arms
of the new world.

Through caring, caressing, and time spent, there is almost a cosmic bond created between mother and daughter. And the daughter learns, ever so gently, about life. The values of trust, and steadfastness, the traits of loyalty, tenderness - all these and more somehow conveyed through the love and connection of a mother and a daughter.

Who knew? Who knew that we women were given a role model from which to establish a vantage point–to be welcomed into the world and experience a seamless transfer of ancient lore from one generation to the other. It is the silent language of love, the language of unconditionality, that allows us as small children to relax into the magnificence of our mother's arms and just be... to absorb... to learn... see... hear... touch... feel... taste... sense.

I know that the experts say that children do not have any memories before 3 years old. Yet there are things we have learned from our parents which defy logic, which stump the most experienced of experts. There must be memories, for there is no other explanation.

Just at the end of my ridiculously tumultuous teens, I remember having a conversation with my cousin who had grown up with my mother. He said that I was so like my mother, the way I walked, the way I held my head, the way I fidgeted - I was so like her that it hurt him to be with me. The resemblance in mannerisms, even the tone of my voice, evoked my mother, and he missed her so. What a magnificent compliment - yet how did I learn all of that? How could I have known?

My mother passed away on the anniversary of my 23rd month. In a time when tragedies happened to "other families" and single parenting just didn't happen, my father was left with a 2-year-old, and I was left with my father. And magnificent memories of my mother... the memories of my mother are alive and well.

My mother, in all her magnificence, taught me, through the brief time we had together, how to laugh, how to sing with joy, how to trust, how to support, and how to love. In such a short time. In such a brief flicker of breath. And in an instant she was gone.

Now I am certain that I really know my mother after all.

—Gail Rosenthal

I Once Gave Them Life

Does fifty years of motherhood lessen the hold on your heart that daughters can have? No. Never!

But it hasn't always been easy. The "hold" that they had sometimes felt awful. I remember when my daughters were teenagers. I was a frustrated mother engaging in hurtful arguments. What were the arguments about: What they could or couldn't do? Where they could or couldn't go? What they should or shouldn't wear? Whatever they were, we seemed to be at loggerheads a lot of the time. And in my frustration, I just blurted out, "Let's face it, we'll just never get along." I'm so glad that proved to not be true. Now, we're the best of friends.

When one calls, and she's not well, you want to "fix it". And when she's unsure with the challenges of motherhood, herself, you try to reassure her. When she's in pain, you'd gladly take it on yourself. When she wants something, and it's not in her budget, you wish for her, abundance. When she and her husband are out of sorts, you want for her perfect harmony.

I was fairly newly married… married three weeks before I turned nineteen.

Over a year had gone by, and thinking it would be wonderful to have a baby, and still not pregnant, I went to my gynecologist. He gave me a ninety-nine cent prescription for hormone tablets, and within no time, I was pregnant. I nibbled crackers in the morning for a few months. I continued to work by jumping on a train and commuting to downtown Detroit. I worked until two weeks before the baby was due - December first. But December first came and went. It was two weeks later, December fifteenth, when I woke up, had pains, left the house, then stopped at my in-laws on the way to the hospital. I sat leisurely and nonchalantly having toast, not wanting to be one of those first-time mothers who went anxiously to the hospital, only to have it be a false alarm, then be sent home by the doctor.

It wasn't a false alarm. Two hours after arriving at the hospital, I gave birth to a healthy girl, seven pounds, nine ounces. That was a pretty good size baby for the skinny one that I was, barely weighing 110 lbs before pregnancy on my 5'7" frame. Coming out of the anesthetic,

I praised the doctor and the nurses, and thanked them profusely for producing such a wonderful miracle, as if they had produced this baby themselves. "You guys are great! Thank you! Thank You! You're so wonderful!!"

Remarried, and ten years later, it took more than a ninety-nine cent pill to get me pregnant with Kristen. It took, beyond the obvious, waiting, and a miscarriage, and a premature delivery. The happy result was the same... awe, wonder, and thankfulness for this life that was created.

I marvel at conception and development, and birth, and at the heredity of features, personality and appearance. It is beyond explaining anything as mysterious and complicated in design.

When motherhood comes upon us, though we are young, and have no prior training to prepare us, and without any practice to give us confidence, we seem to rise to the occasion, though imperfectly and dubiously.

In the nineteen- fifties, with my first child, Grandpa and Grandma, Great Grandpa and Grandma and loving in-laws, shared in my enthusiasm and joy. But how was I supposed to go to the grocery store? How was I supposed to leave the house? Boiling bottles in the 'fifties, and washing diapers, and making formula on the stove was a common routine. We felt extravagant when we purchased disposable diapers and store-bought formula to travel with, things that are common now.

Motherhood has outlasted Missus-hood. The marriage didn't last. Motherhood did. And always will.

I was a single mother thru some of their growing up years, trying to work, and have my girls properly cared for. Anxiety and guilt were common feelings. And you know that your children didn't always "get it" that you loved them unconditionally.

I would take back the days of my children's birth and growing up years in a heartbeat. I would be eye to eye with them more. I would clean the house less, play with them more, talk with them more, holler less, you know... do all the things we wish we had done.

For me, Motherhood is heart-filling in a way no other relationship can be. There's a connection that outlasts all other relationships.

What other role would have us rising in the middle of the night, changing poopy diapers, creaming their chapped butts, and letting them suckle from the breast until it's bloody? Who else would be singing silly songs, talking baby talk, making contorted faces, ice skating in 20 degree weather, sewing ballerina costumes, urging them out onto the stage at a recital, listening to a two hour elementary school concert of stringed instruments, sour notes and all? Who in their right mind at age forty-one would ride the Magic Mountain at Disney World, and be totally unaware of the harrowing ride because you're comforting your terrorized child.

We curtail our own desires to buy something, in order to buy them skiis. We mop up vomit, while we're trying not to throw up ourselves. We graciously make breakfast, when we could hardly get out of bed. We fight their battles for them when they're falsely accused. We try to boost their self-esteem when they unfavorably compare themselves to others. We relinquish our car to them when they receive their driver's license. We spend thousands of dollars to send them to college, only to wrestle with them to stay in college. We help them do homework when we're feeling stupid ourselves, afraid they know. We worry that they won't be "included," and then we worry that they will, but in the wrong crowd. We hide the hurt we feel when they are humiliated and embarrassed.

We do all this, knowing we can't escape being thought the "critical parent." I know, a lot of mothers probably feel like they'll be glad when they're out of a job, when their kids are grown up and gone. But that job is one I would take back in a heartbeat, and enjoy it to the max.

But, I don't need to be melancholic. I can now watch my daughters raise their children, and see why a mother can get derailed from just sitting and playing and stroking their kids as they grow. A lot of what I see, as I watch them, is about washing, folding, and putting away laundry endlessly, keeping the house furnished with supplies, and cleaned, and organized, and meals planned, and groceries shopped for and brought into the house, and meals cooked. Once you cook for them, and serve them, you have to try to get them to EAT. Then meals have to be cleaned up afterwards, and dishes done and put away.

Even in the best of homes, there's siblings fighting, and peace that you strive to maintain. Baths have to be given or taken, and teeth brushed, and prayers said, and kids tucked into bed, hopefully, peacefully. And it isn't always - peaceful, that is.

There are the inevitable accidents and injuries, and emergency hospital visits. And, "is your homework done," is a daily question. Grades have to be monitored. Teachers have to be heard, behavior has to be handled, transportation has to be provided for - to ballet, or ballgames, choir or bowling, soccer or church. Braces have to be tightened, hair has to be cut, (sometimes even de-liced - depending on the friends they hang out with); measles and mumps have to be doctored and dealt with.

I know I've sounded sentimental for the good ole days.

On second thought, I think I'll just enjoy my two daughters, and a job well done with them, and watch proudly from afar as they try their hand at motherhood. I can pull up a chair and pop in a DVD and watch nostalgically fifty years of pictures from the past, turn off the DVD and enjoy new experiences in the present, and dream of making wonderful memories for the future... daughters and grandchildren, all.

They are at the heart of my emotions and affections.
I once gave them life.
Now, they give me life

—Emma Lavonne

Keeping Your Balance

STAYING CONNECTED TO YOUR ENERGY

My 15 year old son came home from school quite upset and not willing to talk about it, which is enough to test any parent's ability to remain in his or her own energy. About 20 minutes later he came to me sobbing. He was under a lot of stress at school and was disappointed in his performance on his swim team. It felt to him as if everything were crashing down on him at once. As I listened to him, I could feel all sorts of emotions running through my body and slowly found myself slipping into his energy. I was feeling a bit scared, frustrated and angry. (Just to name a few) I spoke to him with as much compassion and understanding that I could find and when he didn't seem to accept any of what I was sharing, I fell into a miserable mood and was absolutely no use to him, only to find myself losing my patience. At that moment, I told him it would be better if he left me alone for a while since anything I said didn't seem to make a difference.

He went back to his room while I sat on the couch completely amazed at how, in just a matter of minutes, I went from being so happy to being so miserable. In that moment I realized that I allowed myself to disconnect from my inner being, ultimately letting another person's energy become mine. I knew in my heart that the only way I could be of help to my son and myself, was to get centered and maintain my inner strength.

I brought myself back to a good feeling place by remembering other times with my son that brought us both, great joy. As I remembered those moments I also remembered more difficult times he has experienced and how he came through those unscathed without my advice.

Once I felt strong again and knew I could be happy regardless of his emotional state I was grateful to have the choice to feel how I wanted to feel no matter what was taking place outside of me. With that clarity I was able to go into his room, tell him I love him and let him know he could continue to focus on his lousy feelings or look beyond the moment to search for some solutions. The choice was his and I didn't have to be a part of it. I then kissed him and left his room knowing that was all I had to do to keep me feeling good.

Although it really does feel like you are at the mercy of other people's emotions, you can absolutely stay in an energy that serves you best. You don't have to get on the emotional roller coaster with them. When you allow yourself to become more of an observer in any given situation you free yourself from believing you are being personally attacked or that you need to solve their stuff. It helps you remember they are speaking from their truth and it doesn't necessarily represent your truth. When you know who you are, how you want to feel and that you really do want the highest good for all involved, you create an energetic vibration that can move from you to them, ultimately changing the outcome of any situation allowing you to walk away feeling good that you stayed connected to your energy.

And in case you're wondering, my son shifted his energy beautifully, gaining new insights and greater strengths along the way.

—Linda Salazar, Certified Personal Life Coach, Author, Speaker
www.AwakenTheGenieWithin.com

Kid's Rules for Life

Never trust a dog to watch your food.
—Patrick, Age 10

When you want something expensive, ask your grandparents.
—Matthew, Age 12

Wear a hat when feeding seagulls.
—Rocky, Age 9

Never try to hide a piece of broccoli in a glass of milk.
—Rosemary, Age 7

Never bug a pregnant mom.
—Nicholas, Age 11

Don't ever be too full for dessert.
—Kelly, Age 10

When your dad is mad and asks you, "Do I look stupid?"
don't answer him.
—Heather, Age 16

Never tell your mom her diet's not working.
—Michael, Age 14

When you get a bad grade in school, show it to mom
when she's on the phone.
—Alyesha, Age 13

Never try to baptize a cat.
—Laura, Age 13

Beware of cafeteria food when it looks like it's moving.
—Rob, Age 10

Never tell your little brother that you're not going to do
what your mom told you to do.
—Hank, Age 12

Never dare your little brother to paint the family car.
—Phillip, Age 13

Lessons Learned

MAMA WAS RIGHT

I've learned to love saying, "Mama was right."

Perhaps like yours, my Mama was simply amazing! She was a single parent raising four kids, working odd jobs just to make ends meet. Yet, from her meager earnings, she always found something to give to somebody. Many times it was a cake to a neighbor. Sometimes it was a few dollars to a needy friend. One time she gave away a pair of my Levi jeans to the neighborhood bully... and I was still in them.

I remember saying, "Mama, why do you always give people stuff? You never get anything." She leaned back in her legs, squared her shoulders, looked me in the eyes and said, "The giver is always rewarded." I said, "The giver is always rewarded? Well how much?" With a slight smile she said, "That's your lesson to learn."

I didn't understand that then but, three moments in my life helped me to understand that "Mama was right. The giver is always rewarded."

The first moment happened while I was giving a speech. I help up a $5 bill and said, "This $5 bill goes to the first person who will bring me three $1 bills." Yeah, I know, my wife thought I was crazy too. Out of 300 people, guess how many had the courage to come forward? One! After my speech she came up to me and asked if I wanted the $5 back. I thought I should say, "Of course I do. I'm not crazy!" But instead I said, "You earned it for having the courage to step forward."

I thought about her a month later when I sat in a university audience listening to this great speaker named Lenny Dave speak on creativity. He held up a book titled, "Making College Count." Ironically, I had planned to buy this book over the internet for my daughter who was entering her first year of college. Lenny said, "Who wants this book?" Everybody raised their hand. Then he said, "Who really, really, really wants this book?" Everybody shouted out, "I do." Everybody but me. I jumped out of my seat, rushed the stage, grabbed the book out of Lenny's hand, ran back to my seat and sat down. Lenny said, "Now he really wanted that book!"

Then he said, "Turn to page 50." I flipped over to page 50. Guess what I found? A $10 bill! Hallelujah! Mama was right!

The second moment happened while on my weekly walk. I see a dime on the sidewalk. To this thrifty engineer, this was like hitting the lotto! I pick it up, shove it in my pocket and continue to walk. Ten minutes later, out of the corner of my eye I see this shabbily dressed homeless woman with her hand out. Our eyes meet and I see more than her appearance. I see someone's daughter, a wife, a mother... who somehow has lost her way.

Out of respect I want to give her something. But all I have is... this thin dime. Touched by something, I place the dime in her hand. With a tear in her eye and a smile on her face she says, "Thank you. Most people ignore me."

A week later I walk pass the same spot looking for the woman. I want to give her something but she's not there. Imagine how I felt when I looked down and see on the sidewalk... a dollar bill! Now I can't explain this, but...Hallelujah! Mama was right again! "The giver is always rewarded."

The third moment happened while I was sitting at home... flipping a coin to see which lucky bill gets paid this month. The phone rang. It was my oldest brother. He asked to borrow a large sum of money. I was struggling under my own burdens. I didn't need his. For some reason...I pushed the house note aside and wrote him a check. Then I sat back and said, "Come on reward... make Mama right again!"

But, this time the reward would come in a different way... a card from my brother. He wrote, "Thank you for being so nice. You and your kindness will be remembered often. This helps me out with my medicine. Love Alton." This card was priceless! It was an act of gratitude under trying circumstances. You see, my brother later lost his gallant fight with cancer. Suddenly, I understood the lyrics, "He ain't heavy, he's my brother."

But more than that, I understood the lesson I needed to learn. It is simply this; the true reward of giving is not about the money you feel in your hand. It is about the moments you feel in your heart!

Like: a moment of courage in the face of fear; a moment of joy to replace a tear; a moment of gratitude... even when death is near. Oh yes! I love saying "Mama was right!" "The giver is always rewarded!"

—James Tucker
Dedicated to Annie Mae Tucker

EDUCATION IS MORE VALUABLE THAN MARRIAGE

Long long ago in 1964, there was a little girl of who had just graduated from high school. The girl had lost her father two years ago. The mother had two older daughters (both married) two older sons - one in college another in high school, the girl was me, and I had one younger brother and sister both in elementary school at that time. My mother raised five children all under 18 years all by herself. She deserves to be on a golden pedestal.

When I think of my mother, tenacity and determination comes to my mind. She had a dream, a principle and had a single pointed focus to fulfill her commitment in raising her children.

"Education for girls is more valuable than their marriage"- my mother said 40 years ago and I agree. In those days, in India, girls were married off very soon. Education for a girl was a luxury and was thought as an additional expense. Girls were considered a liability but my mother was very different. My mother had a strong conviction that girls must be educated to the maximum possible so that they are independent and able to stand on their own feet. She dreamt that her children, each one of us would go to college and get at least a degree.

As a young girl, after losing my father, I wanted to make my mother happy because I knew she was always right. The family members were against it. My uncles and aunts had very strong opposition to my mother's ideas. They tried to take control of raising her children as she had lost her husband. They felt it was their responsibility to help this family.

My mother was very intelligent and she handled the situation very diplomatically. Not hurting anyone in the family, she argued her point, and asked me to get admission in a local college in the subject that I liked. In four years, I graduated with Honors from the university.

Again, it was time to get into workforce. I was not allowed to work. This time, my mother lost the battle with the family members but she knew that with the given conditions, she did her best. I was married to a very loving and devoted person. The youngest in the family, my sister, got her Masters degree and I am proud to say that she is a college professor. She was also married to an Engineer.

My college education helped me to take up and move on the corporate ladder faster when my husband passed away and I chose to do what my mother did to me. I focused on educating my daughters.

One of them is a surgeon and the other an adult educator.

My mother strongly felt that all children could be in their best.
Her three sons have doctoral degree and not to mention their
children are very highly qualified.

Without the strong will power of my loving mother who was
educated only up to 8th grade and married at the age of twelve I
wonder
where all of us would be now! She passed away two years ago but
her words will always sound in my ears "Education for girls is more
valuable than their marriage."

—Vijaya Jayaraman
Dedicated to my mother, Neeloo Krishnamurti, Bombay, India
Note: English is my second language.

WHAT I LEARNED ABOUT LIFE FROM MY MOTHER

When I reflect upon lessons learned and most common phrases from
my mother, these rise to the top of the list:

1) "Know what you want in life - and go for it."
A child of the Depression, at 18, Mom moved herself from the farm in
Iowa, with only $10, and her best girlfriend to "get a life" in California.
I was named after that best girlfriend.

2) "You can do anything you put your mind to."
A secret dream of Mom was to compete in the Olympics. Although
it wasn't possible, she did receive the Volunteer of the Year award at
the Olympic Training Center in San Diego for tireless hours of hosting
tours, and working with the athletes before the Games. At 68, her
color photo made the front page of the local newspaper, carrying the
Olympic Torch, on its way from San Diego to the Los Angeles Games.

3) "Stay healthy. Life is too short to get sick."
Three days after my parents' 50th wedding anniversary, mom went to
have chest pains checked out, and was admitted to emergency for
clogged arteries. While in the ICU, she pleaded "Sheryl, you've got to
come get me. I'm okay! There are some really sick people in here!"

—Sheryl Lynn Roush
Dedicated to Beverly Joyce Roush, a most persistent woman

SHE TAUGHT US HOW TO LIVE

Our Momma, born Christmas Day 1909, was the organizer and head of our family of seven. Our father was disabled and Mom kept us all busy growing vegetables, raising rabbits and chickens and going to school. To earn extra money Momma Helen started a wakeup service. She taught us resourcefulness.

Life was hard but she always seemed happy and that was infectious. She shared anything we had and so many people called her Momma Helen that sometimes we would feel jealous, and a little proud. She enjoyed helping people and always had some loving advice. She taught us to love and share.

When Dad died it was as if Momma's life ended and started at the same moment. She was able to do so much more and yet we would find her crying quietly by herself. She taught us personal strength.

When she was in her late seventies she had a mild stoke and was unable to walk. When she had another stroke and lost her ability to speak. She would watch a person in the room and smile. Sometimes she would work out a "thank you" or "please" to the nurses and doctors. She continued to fade into the world of Alzheimer's and the final six years she was unable to do anything for herself. She taught us acceptance.

A few days before her 89th birthday Momma passed away, quietly.

Her funeral services were held on Christmas Eve afternoon. As busy as everyone was at that time of year, people came from many miles, some traveled for a few days to get here and others came that never knew her personally (they had heard the stories).

Maybe the best tribute of all was the six nurses that had taken care of Momma for so many years, took off work and drove more than 70 miles to attend her funeral. They said it best when they said "Momma Helen" as they passed her casket. That day we were able to stop being jealous and be only proud. She taught us to how to live a good life.

—Jack Nichols (big brother), and Judy Tejwani (little sister)
Dedicated to their mother, Momma Helen Nichols

Life

Love is seeing and feeling life everywhere.
When your heart is full of love, you sense life pulsating through
all creation. You do not grow tired when there is love.
Love is the natural attitude of the soul; it expresses the heart's
longing for Divinity. You can only feel love by expressing it.
—Amma (Mother), Mata Amritanandamayi, India
Messages from Amma: In the Language of the Heart, www.amma.org

The rules of a happy life are these:
Smile, Have Fun, and Be wild and Crazy.
Risk ridicule and enjoy the moment.
—Cynthia Brian, Speaker, Author *Chicken Soup for the Gardener's Soul*

Life would be so much easier if we just had the Source Code.
—*Bumper Sticker*

Acting happier than you feel can make you happier than you are.
—Fran Lebowitz

Enthusiasm is at the heart of any positive change in the world.
Each of us have something to offer to uplift the spirit of others,
whether through achieving a lifelong goal that inspires children to
make better choices, influencing friends to a healthier way of life,
helping people heal themselves, creating a joyful workplace or home,
or connecting more deeply with family, nature, or a cause. In all of
its expressions, enthusiasm is a gift to be shared with the world.
—Mary Marcdante, Speaker, Author *Living with Enthusiasm*
www.MaryMarcdante.com

Bring love into this day. The present moment is all we have,
and all we will ever have, and it is where we find the joy and
power of God's presence.
—Mary Manin Morrissey, Author *Life Keys*

While we have the gift of life, it seems to me the only tragedy
is to allow part of us to die whether it is our spirit,
our creativity or our glorious uniqueness.
—Gilda Radner

Mothers are the bearers of life, the caretakers of our children, the
light of our future.
—Catherine Tilley

"Modeh Ani"
"I am grateful before you."
These are the first words you are to say in the morning
in traditional Jewish life.
—Linda Kaplan Spitz, MD

Life is not measured by the number of breaths we take
but by the moments that take our breath away.
—Unknown

The more you praise and celebrate your life,
 the more there is in life to celebrate.
—Oprah Winfrey

Loss & Grieving

BEYOND THE SKY

Much like the sun and moon or tide
Memories can never die.
Those we love dwell forever there
In distant mists and evening air.
That is where your loved ones wait
Beyond the clouds, pleasant state
So do not grieve that they've gone there
To a place of the seasons always fair.
Heal knowing you can join them someday.
Let not let grief stand in your way,
Since if your loved one's in your heart,
You'll never really have to part.
For in a place just 'round the bend,
You will surely meet again,
Where in the fog and evening air,
All our loved ones will be there.

And we will all meet again.

—Rosalie Ferrer Kramer, Speaker, Poet, Author—
www.authorsden.com/rosaliefkramer

Sorrow is the teacher that brings you closer to God.
—Amma (Mother), Mata Amritanandamayi, India
Messages from Amma: In the Language of the Heart, www.amma.org

Time is the only comforter for the loss of a mother.
—Jane Welsh Carlyle

Poets have said that the reason to have children is to give yourself immortality. Immortality? Now that I have five children, my only hope is that they are all out of the house before I die.
—Bill Cosby, Comedian

We understand death for the first time when he
puts his hand upon one whom we love.
—Madame de Stael

When you are sorrowful look again in your heart,
and you shall see that in truth you are weeping
for that which has been your delight.
—Kahlil Gibran

What soap is for the body, tears are for the soul.
—Jewish Proverb

God is closest to those with broken hearts.
—Jewish Proverb

Hope is the feeling you have that the feeling you have isn't
permanent.
—Jean Kerr

Those who do not know how to weep with their whole heart
don't know how to laugh either.
—Golda Meir

God made death so we'd know when to stop.
—Steven Stiles

Whenever someone you know dies, or makes their transition,
I believe you now have angels that you know.
—Oprah Winfrey

Maybe part of loving is learning to let go.
—From the TV series *The Wonder Years*

God can heal a broken heart, but He has to have all the pieces.
—Unknown

LOVING ARMS
A song written for Karl's Mom before she died in 1993

Please if you must go, then let me know...
where will I feel your loving arms
Is it too much to want for the touch... I have been used to all my life
I am afraid, a decision is made... but I am less than willing
So if you must go, then let me know...
where will I feel your loving arms

Please could you disguise or look through the eyes...
used by a perfect stranger
Then, whether or not, this lesson is taught...
I will be in your loving arms
In all that I do, I'm thinking of you... and it will bless my life
So please, if you must go, then let me know...
please let me feel your loving arms

I am afraid a decision is made... and I am less than willing...
so if you must go, then let me know...
where will I feel your loving arms
If you must go, then let me know...
please let me feel your.... loving arms
Here is where I will feel your... loving arms

—Karl Anthony, Singer, Author, Songwriter
www.KarlAnthony.com

It's What Women Do

A friend of mine recently lost her 10 year old daughter. Needless to say, her grief was profound. The remarkable love shown by her friends compelled me to write a short poem for her and her closest friends. Their friendship came alive, as though one was watching a beautifully choreographed dance of love and commitment. Their loyalty and sense of protection showed the strength and endurance of a rock that has long parted a rushing stream. One of them was broken; that she would heal was never in question. They are the healers. This is their art. They are women. It is what women do.
—Mary Jo Harte, R.N., Speaker

At 17 years old I was a student nurse in the nursery; this was the mid-60's – when nurses were mean to their younger co-workers. I was told to take a dead 3-day-old baby to the morgue that was seven floors below the nursery. On my way down as I held this dead baby in my arms, a major epiphany occurred. What came to me: Life was short and I need to make the most of each day. As a result of that event, I have lived my life to the utmost.

To this day I have only one regret – that I didn't see Elvis Presley do a live show.

Many people question why do babies or young children die. My take is they die to teach us lessons and my lesson changed my life dramatically as well as other people who are part of my life.

To this day, I will never forget the event; I thank the baby for only one regret in my life.

To this day is my life this was the most dramatic and memorable event in my whole life!

—Gloria J. VanDam, RN

I DID NOT DIE

Do not stand by my grave and grieve.
I am not there, I did not leave.
For I'm that distant shining star.
I'm all around you, never far.
I'm the sparkle in children's eyes.
I paint the blue in the autumn skies.
And in those cool sweet summer eves,
I hide in shadows the sunshine weaves.
Together we did laugh and cry,
But now I'm ever at your side.
For long as I am in your heart,
We will never really part.
So live your life and do be gay,
And look forward to that day,
When somewhere just around the bend,
We will surely meet again.

—Rosalie Ferrer Kramer, Speaker, Poet, Author—

My Mama, My Sweet Pea

Thinking about you now,
I feel the great love and dignity that was you.
It was simple, It was pure.
Present, even in your sleep.
You were my baby these past months.
No other reward could have meant so much to me Mama.
My devotion to you.
It was simple. It was pure. It was a God thing.
I fed you, I held you, I made you laugh.
Nothing else mattered.
Oh, thank you Mama.

You gave me life
then I held yours in the palm of my hands
until you let it go.
Goodbye Mama, Goodbye.
How I love you.
You are forever in my heart.

— Cassandra Northington —

Dear Sweet Mama

So tired and weary and loved by all,
One year ago Mama answered God's call.
Rosie, sweet Rosie, come rest in my arms,
Fly with the Angels and fear ye no harm.
We'll not surrender to our sorrow or give in to the pain,
Forever in our memories dear sweet Mama will remain.
God shows His tender mercy and comforts us each day,
Our strength lies in the love of God and His promise is our way.
We'll cherish the love Mama gave us until we meet again,
God blessed us with our Mama who we'll love until the end.
We miss her gentle heart and soul but God knows what is best,
God has her in His loving care and took her Home to rest.
We miss dear sweet Mama's love, her smile and precious touch,
God bless our dear sweet Mama who we love and miss so much.

— Judith A. Duran —

In Celebration of A Life

My heart is still trying to heal, and it's been a year. Some days the joy I feel at remembering our time together overpowers the grief I feel at losing him to death. At the end, living in Las Vegas in his declining condition, he told me, "Mom, we don't have to be in the same room to be together."

Here on earth my heart is flooded with memories of you beginning with your birth, when in the arms of the assisting nurse, you scowled down at me, still attached to the umbilical cord, crying like a little warrior. My little warrior! Your scowl turned to smiles and even to gleeful laughter in those nightly romps before your 10 PM feeding when your Dad holding you high in the air with arms extended 'dive-bombed' you around and around, up and down swooping you toward me.

Of my million memories of you, these come to mind today:

At 17 months you said your first sentence at bedtime to your Dad, "I'm going nighty-night, good-bye."

Then at 3, in a heavy downpour you informed me that someone forgot to turn off the water.

And after every hug, you'd say, "Mommy, I love you all the much in the world."

I remember the ruined Thanksgiving when you were 4 and claimed the live Turkey for a pet and wouldn't eat a bite when we cooked it for our dinner. You had such a tender heart.

Once after taking too long to come home from school you said, "I took the long-cut home."

Your happy face when we came for you after a week at Summer Camp... your shaved head on the football team and we called you Mr. Clean... trying on your Dad's Marine Corps dress blues... your accomplishments on writing your book... and fathering Pamela.

My wise, brave warrior, you faced life with courage and joy and that gives me joy and courage too. The world is a better place for having had you in it. I love you all the much in the world.

Mom
—Norma Kipp Avendano, mother
A tribute to her son, Charles Eric Kipp, who passed January 12, 2005

WHEN YOUR MOTHER PASSES

You hold her hand impossibly tight,
Listening, listening, with all of your might,
You want to hear, just once more for you,
"I love you, and I'm proud of all that you do.

Instead, she struggles for each last breath,
Her eyes closed tight – her body near death.
You want to hold her, but you're afraid she'll break,
How can she leave you? So much of you she'll take.

You wait for a signal – some kind of sign,
That she'll be all right for the rest of time.
You know she needs approval from you,
That it's all right to go away from view.

Her breath grows more labored,
You wonder what to do.
Who will tell you, "I'm so proud of you."
Who will remember from day one?
Where will your memories go, when her life is done?

The hour is near, she's grown so tired.
She did her job – she served her time.
She needs to know it's her last day.
She needs to know that you'll be okay.

It's so hard, you take a break.
The day is still, your body does ache.
You sit down next to the open door,
The curtains blow – you're alone no more.

The angels have come to take her away.
"I know you're here, talk to me," you say.
Her breathing changes – soft as a baby.
Is it Daddy or Grandma she sees? Well, maybe.

You grab her hand You grab her hand and know it's time.
The words must come – the words sublime.
I'll be okay, Mom, it's okay to go,
You'll always be with me – I love you so.

It's okay to go,
You'll always be with me – I love you so.
Within seconds your dear mother breathes no more,
Her body is there, but her spirit does soar.
Her soul has moved on and you're all alone,
"Mom is gone," you cry, "now she'll never phone."

You do the right thing to see her off to eternity,
The proper casket, ceremony and serendipity.
Your body's empty, you have no heart,
Your mother's gone – She bore your start.

How can you live without the womb,
That was your first and most loving room?
Where is the meaning when Mom is dead?
Who will you try to make happy instead?

Days and months pass by like sand,
You cry and cry and search the land.
Who will love you unconditionally?
"No one," you say, "Its up to me."

Now you can do it because Mom's moved in,
She lives in your heart where she's Mother Hen.
You'll never be lonely – you're living for two,
Moms never leave, they just become you.

—Judith Parker Harris, Speaker—
Author of Master Challenges in Your Life
and Move From Blocked to Block-Buster
www.blockedtoblock-buster.com

Love

Love is patient, love is kind. It does not envy, it does not boast, it is not proud. It is not rude, it is not self-seeking, it is not easily angered, it keeps no record of wrongs. Love does not delight in evil but rejoices with the truth. It always protects, always trusts, always perseveres. Love never fails. But where there are prophecies, they will cease; where there are tongues, they will be stilled; where there is knowledge, it will pass away... And now these things remain: faith, hope and love. But the greatest of these is love.
—1 Corinthians 13:1-8, 13

As the body needs food to survive and grow, the soul needs love. Love instills a strength and vitality that even mother's milk cannot provide. All of us live and long for real love. We are born and die searching for such love. Children, love each other and unite in pure love.
—Amma (Mother), Mata Amritanandamayi, India
Messages from Amma: In the Language of the Heart, www.amma.org

Love is the face of God.
—Amma (Mother), Mata Amritanandamayi, www.amma.org

Love is that condition in the human spirit so profound that it allows me to survive, and better than that, to thrive with passion, compassion, and style.
—Maya Angelou, American poet, writer, and actress

Love. What is love? No word can define it, it's something so great, only God could design it. Yes, love is beyond, what man can define, for love is immortal, and God's gift is Divine.
—Anonymous

Love is, above all, the gift of oneself.
—Jean Anouilh

I love you not only for what you are, but for what I am when I am with you. I love you not only for what you have made of yourself, but for what you are making of me. I love you for the part of me that you bring out.
—Elizabeth Barrett Browning, English poet

You never lose by loving. You always lose by holding back.
—Barbara De Angelis, Speaker, Author

Nobody has ever measured, even poets, how much a heart can hold.
—Zelda Fitzgerald

You learn to love by loving.
—Anatole France, French writer, Nobel Prizes for Literature

Where there is love there is life.
—Indira Gandhi, Indian Prime Minister

Never let a problem to be solved
become more important than the person to be loved.
—Barbara Johnson, Best-selling writer

Thru mysterious means, love travels...
into closed hearts and opens them. Eventually.
—Cath Kachur, Speaker, Artist, www.HumanTuneUp.com

Start living now. Stop saving the good china for that special occasion. Stop withholding your love until that special person materializes. Every day you are alive is a special occasion. Every minute, every breath, is a gift from God.
—Mary Manin Morrissey, Author *Life Keys*

Your task is not to seek for love, but merely to seek
and find all the barriers within yourself that you have built against it.
—Djalal ad-Din Rumi, Persian Mystic and Poet, 1207-1273

There is nothing more important in life than love.
—Barbra Streisand

Little children look right through that which we have learned to be
and into the beauty of our soul. This is truly love.
—Catherine Tilley, www.theglobalvoice.com

There are four questions of value in life...
What is sacred?
Of what is the spirit made?
What is worth living for, and what is worth dying for?
The answer to each is the same.
Only love.
—Unknown

Just because somebody doesn't love you the way you want them to,
doesn't mean they don't love you with all they have.
—Unknown

Love is to let those we love be perfectly themselves,
and not to twist them to fit our own image...
otherwise we love only the reflection of ourselves we find in them.
—Unknown

Love is saying "I feel differently" instead of "You're wrong."
—Unknown

Love isn't finding a perfect person.
It's seeing an imperfect person perfectly.
—Unknown

The spiritual meaning of love is measured by what it can do.
Love is meant to heal. Love is meant to renew.
Love is meant to bring us closer to God.
—Unknown

If you give your life as a wholehearted response to love,
then love will wholeheartedly respond to you.
Love is the intuitive knowledge of our hearts.
—Marianne Williamson, Author *A Woman's Worth*

Loving Yourself

You yourself, as much as anybody in the entire universe,
deserve your love and affection.
—Buddha

Finding your passion is connecting the dots between your head
and your heart.
—Maria Marsala, www.ElevatingYou.com

When you find peace within yourself, you could become the kind
of person who can live at peace with others.
—*Peace Pilgrim*

You teach people who you are by the way you treat yourself.
—Lynn Pierce, Author *Change One Thing, Change Your Life*
www.ChangeOneThing.com

It isn't until you come to a spiritual understanding of who you are-
not necessarily a religious feeling, but deep down, the spirit within-
that you can begin to take control.
—Oprah Winfrey

Declare today "sacred time"—off-limits to everyone,
unless invited by you.
Take care of your personal wants and needs.
Say no, graciously but firmly, to others' demands.
—Oprah Winfrey

Affirmations for Honoring Ourselves

I am a valued human being.
I am always treated with respect.
I am empowered.
I am supportive of other women.
I easily speak up for myself.
I deserve to have boundaries.
My boundaries are respected.
I make waves whenever I need to.
I have a good support team.
I have integrity.
The more open I am, the safer I am.
I am a woman healing other women.
I have a strong energy barrier.
The men in my life honor women.
I take my power back.
I love and honor myself.

—Louise L. Hay—
Author *Empowering Women*

Learning to Love Yourself

Love yourself exactly as you are, and you are forever changed
Love everything you can from wherever you find yourself
Think of someone you love a lot, and love yourself that much
When you forget how to love yourself, love yourself for forgetting
Jump from logic into the safety net of love
Open your love big enough to fit all your feelings
Say, "I can love myself for that" too!
Love others exactly as they are, and they are free to change.

—Kathlyn & Gay Hendricks—
Conscious Loving

LOVE YOURSELF AS THY NEIGHBOR

I am a health care professional with 30 years experience.
I am always perplexed and amazed how women in particular look
after everybody so well. So why do they forget themselves?

Our main purpose is to look after ourselves including our physical,
mental and spiritual selves. On many occasion I have had friends
and strangers say you really know who to look after your self and
I take it as a compliment with grace.

I pray for all women in this world to realize their most important job
is to care for their physical, mental and spiritual needs. When your
needs are met, you will discover you have more love, energy and
desire to help as many people as you chose. You will do things –
for other people from the heart, not obligation, resentment, anger
or self-pity.

You say, "How do I start?"
That is easy – start with the first step saying to yourself,
"I love myself."

Then take some action steps.
Your question is, "What action steps?"

Each of us is different.
Here are a few things that work for me: time alone, walks,
meditation, massage, facials, friends and family.

Just remember when you say yes to a request make sure it is really
what you WANT to do.

"Yes" pleases other people and "No" pleases you.
Learn the art of saying "No" without feeling guilty and
love yourself as thy neighbour.

—Gloria J. Van Dam, RN

Making a Difference

Everyone needs to be valued.
Everyone has the potential to give something back.
—Diana, Princess of Wales

Extend love. Help the world work.
—Cath Kachur, Speaker, Author, Artist

Never doubt that a small group of thoughtful,
committed citizens can change the world.
Indeed, it's the only thing that ever has.
—Margaret Mead

We can do no great things, only small things with great love.
—Mother Teresa

In politics, if you want anything said, ask a man;
if you want anything done, ask a woman.
—Margaret Thatcher

The true stewardship of a woman lies not in what she has,
but in how she affects the lives of others.
—Rheba Washington-Lindsey, Author *Teaching Isn't For Cowards*

In every community, there is work to be done.
In every nation, there are wounds to heal.
In every heart, there is the power to do it.
—Marianne Williamson, Author *A Woman's Worth*

Devote today to something so daring
even you can't believe you're doing it.
—Oprah Winfrey

Mary, Mother of Jesus

Yes, Lord

Obedient daughter of God

Pure

Gentle

Willing

Open

Strong

Trusting

Prayerful

Prayer - aware

Sensitive

Inconspicuous

Humble

Believing

— Emily B. DeShazo —

A Conversation between Mary, the mother of Jesus and God:

Mary, I want you to do something for me.
Yes, Lord.

Mary, you know I love you and will take care of you.
Yes, Lord.

Mary, what I'm asking won't always be easy.
Yes, Lord.

Mary, I need your whole life dedicated to my one glorious purpose.
Yes, Lord.

Mary, when you are lonely and afraid, I'll be just a heartbeat away.
Yes, Lord.

Mary, I have chosen you of all women because of your pure, obedient love for me.
Yes, Lord.

Mary, I have given you life.
Now I need your help in bringing forth my son's life.
Yes, Lord.
Mary, people won't understand.
They'll hurt your feelings but my hand is on your shoulder.

There will be so much you don't understand but it's alright, I am with you every minute.
Yes, Lord.

Mary, I will send my holy son to earth through you, my blessed daughter.
You will bear him and raise him and teach him.
Yes, Lord.

Mary, I'll be there with you but you will be my earthly hands and feet and heart for him.
Yes, Lord

Mary, I know you care for Joseph. He is part of my plan, too.
Yes, Lord.

Mary, my son will need an earthly father to lead him through
childhood, into boyhood, to teach him a trade
and to help him become a man.
Yes, Lord.

Mary, soon you will go to help your cousin, Elizabeth,
with her pregnancy. She will share yours, too, and you will
comfort and draw womanly strength from each other.
Yes, Lord.

Other family members won't understand.
Just leave them to me.
Yes, Lord.

Mary, dear daughter of mine, just look up.
I am here.
Talk to me every chance you get.
It's okay for you to cry or get discouraged
but not for long because I am with you.
Whether you are facing wild animals, or kings,
or peasants with my son.
I'll be there, too.
Yes, Lord.

The journey of his life will not be easy for you.
From his birth then his boyhood and teenage years,
he will seem to be rebelling against you.
But, remember, he is doing my work and your heart is always in his.
You are the one person on earth who will always
and forever give him unconditional love.
That is your job as His Mother.
Yes, Lord.

Mary, the end of His life will not be the end of His life.
He will be crucified, buried and rise again to live forever -
all eternity.
But first there will be betrayal and heartache and pain for Him.
Do you understand?
NO, Lord.
I am His Mother.

— Emily B. DeShazo —

Mary, Did You Know

Mary, did you know
that your Baby Boy would one day walk on water?
Mary, did you know
that your Baby Boy would save our sons and daughters?
Did you know
that your Baby Boy has come to make you new?
This Child that you delivered will soon deliver you.

Mary, did you know
that your Baby Boy will give sight to a blind man?
Mary, did you know
that your Baby Boy will calm the storm with His hand?
Did you know
that your Baby Boy has walked where angels trod?
When you kiss your little Baby you kissed the face of God?

Mary, did you know...

The blind will see.
The deaf will hear.
The dead will live again.
The lame will leap.
The dumb will speak
The praises of The Lamb.

Mary, did you know
that your Baby Boy is Lord of all creation?
Mary, did you know
that your Baby Boy will one day rule the nations?
Did you know...
that your Baby Boy is heaven's perfect Lamb?
The sleeping Child you're holding is the Great, I Am.

— Christian Song Lyrics —

Submitted by Jessica Nibbs

Materni-Tea

Tea Prayer

I marvel at the miracle of motherhood.
The experience of life within life is clearly understood,
and the power of creation and gestation are like no other.
This I share with the Divine Mother
and I know we are one -
that I am one with all that is.

The intuition of the Divine Mother and
the wisdom of the Divine Feminine are all in me.
And in all women; we are one and the same,
regardless of shape and shade, there is no shame.
There is only good and only God.

In claiming my own good, my heart opens to see the good
of my own offspring and the good of my own mother.
For these maternal bonds and instincts,
I give thanks to the Divine Creator.
For the honour to create and carry life,
there is nothing greater, and I give thanks.

This joy I share with God, the Creator of all life.
And if out of confusion, I allow joy to turn
into frustration or desperation, I remember to surrender,
and I give it all back to the Divine Creator,
and I am reborn.
I let go and go back to God,
Mother-Father God and I am whole again.

Amen

—Darlene Fahl-Brittian—
Certified Tea Specialist
Sipping Tea - Celebrating Me
www.TakeUpTheCup.com

Men!

Ever notice how all of women's problems start with men?
MENtal illness, MENstrual cramps, MENtal breakdown, MENopause.
And when we have real problems, it's HIS-terectomy!
Don't forget the "GUY" necologist!
—Anonymous

Few women admit their age . . .
Fewer men act theirs.
—Bumper Sticker

You see, dear, it is not true that woman was made from man's rib;
she was really made from his funny bone.
—J.M. Barrie, *What Every Woman Knows*

Sometimes I wonder if men and women really suit each other.
Perhaps they should live next door and just visit now and then.
—Katharine Hepburn

I have learned that only two things are necessary to keep
one's wife happy. First, let her think she's having her own way.
And second, let her have it.
—Lyndon B. Johnson, Former President of the United States

Successful marriage is always a triangle: a man, a woman, and God.
—Cecil Myers

Adam and Eve had an ideal marriage.
He didn't have to hear about all the men she could have married,
and she didn't have to hear about the way his mother cooked.
—Unknown

Don't settle for a relationship that won't let you be yourself.
—Oprah Winfrey

WHAT WOMEN SAY ABOUT MEN...

I married beneath me - all women do.
—Nancy Astor, in a speech in England, 1951

A man's got to do what a man's got to do.
A woman must do what he can't.
—Rhonda Hansome

The men in our lives are mirrors of what we believe about ourselves.
So often we look to others to make us feel loved and connected
when all they can do is mirror our own relationship with ourselves.
—Louise L. Hay, Speaker, Author *Empowering Women*

Sometimes you have to get to know someone really well
to realize you're really strangers.
—Mary Tyler Moore, Actress

Can you imagine a world without men?
No crime and lots of happy fat women.
—Marion Smith and Nicole Hollander

A male gynecologist is like an auto mechanic
who has never owned a car.
—Carrie Snow

A man over time falls in love with the woman he is attracted to,
and a woman over time becomes more attracted to the man she
loves.
—Jennifer Wilkinson

A lot of guys think the larger a woman's breasts are,
the less intelligent she is. I don't think it works like that.
I think it's the opposite. I think the larger a woman's breasts are,
the less intelligent the men become.
—Anita Wise

WHAT MEN SAY ABOUT WOMEN...

When you can see your unborn children in her arms,
you know you really love a woman.
—Bryan Adams, Singer, Song Lyrics

To get to a woman's heart, a man must first use his own.
—Mike Dobbertin, quoted in *A 5th Portion of Chicken Soup for the Soul*

A woman should soften but not weaken a man.
—Sigmund Freud

After about 20 years of marriage, I'm finally starting to scratch the
surface of that one. And I think the answer lies somewhere between
conversation and chocolate.
—Mel Gibson, about what women want

The supply of good women far exceeds that of
the men who deserve them.
—Robert Graves

I've reached the age where competence is a turn-on.
—Billy Joel, singer, songwriter

Women really do rule the world. They just haven't figured it out yet.
When they do, and they will, we're all in big big trouble.
—"Doctor" Leon

Women cannot complain about men anymore
until they start getting better taste in them.
—Bill Maher

Every woman needs one man in her life who is strong and
responsible. Given this security, she can proceed to do what she really
wants to do–fall in love with men who are weak and irresponsible.
—Richard J. Needham

Ah, women. They make the highs higher and the lows more
frequent.
—Friedrich Wilhelm Nietzsche

If women didn't exist, all the money in the world
would have no meaning.
—Aristotle Onassis

Every woman is wrong until she cries,
and then she is right - instantly.
—Sam Slick (Thomas Chandler Haliburton)

Real love is when you become selfless and you are more
concerned about your mate's or children's egos than your own.
You're now a giver instead of a taker.
—Sylvester Stallone, Actor, best known as the character "Rocky"

Men never remember, but women never forget.
—Unknown

Women always worry about the things that men forget;
men always worry about the things women remember.
—Unknown

I hate women because they always know where things are.
—Voltaire

Men always want to be a woman's first love -
women like to be a man's last romance.
—Oscar Wilde, Irish poet

God gave us all a penis and a brain,
but only enough blood to run one at a time.
—Robin Williams, Comedian

On the one hand, we'll never experience childbirth.
On the other hand, we can open all our own jars.
—Bruce Willis, on the difference between men and women

Miracle Babies

We're Taking Your Baby to Intensive Care

When my newborn son was laid into my arms after twelve hours of labor, I was so groggy I could scarcely hold him. Sometime during the night, someone came to tell me that he was having trouble breathing, and they were taking him to ICU to keep a closer watch on him. I called my husband, and through my sobs, told him something terrible was happening.

"They said they wanted to take some fluid from his brain, to rule out Cystic Fibrosis because he's having trouble breathing," I blubbered. Pumping, they called the in-and-out motion of his tiny chest.

What! I'd had no problems during pregnancy, no hint that anything could be wrong, except that he was four weeks overdue, and had to be induced. And I smoked.

I tried to quit, but I just couldn't. In 1973 I began hearing warnings to women about the dangers of smoking during pregnancy. We smokers were still scoffers. Afterall, hadn't our parents and grandparents been *encouraged* by their doctors to smoke during pregnancy, to keep their weight down? And, after the baby was born, to take up smoking to lose weight? But those were all excuses, I just couldn't do it, and I didn't appreciate the criticality of quitting. Now look what happened: my baby might die.

The doctors found no indication of CF, but they did have to reinflate one of Danny's partially collapsed lungs, repeatedly. I was never so panicked in my life, convinced that this was my retribution for smoking; my tiny son would pay for it.

When I left Nyack Hospital after three days, Danny stayed behind. I came back and cared for him in ICU all day, every day. He seemed a veritable giant at seven pounds four ounces, and twenty-one inches long, beside a two pound preemie curled up like a snail, struggling for life in the neighboring isolet. I stared at Danny's bare chest above the round little tummy, and watched it drawing up, in and out, struggling for breath, an oxygen tube running down his nose.

The Nixon hearings began to be televised the day Danny was born, May 18, 1973. They droned on and on, as I sat in a wooden chair, holding my tiny baby in my lap or on my shoulder, nearly all the day, while he puked up fountains of one baby food after another. He was colicky, so he screamed much of the time, particularly when I put him down.

Seven weeks crawled by, weeks of reinflating his lungs, risks of infection, and tests. I even got to take him home briefly, but ended up back at the hospital with his faulty breathing, colic and milk allergies. I was an absolute wreck worried that I had done this to my tiny son. Eventually, after a hair raising ambulance ride to New York Hospital with no benefit, the doctor concluded Danny simply had multiple allergies, and I should take him home and get on with life.

I did, and life was very difficult. Though my husband was not making much money in those years of the oil embargo and gas rationing, when interest rates were 15 and 17%, I stayed home with my son. The endless crying and vomiting went on and on, and I was exhausted. I not only washed all his clothes and sheets after the briefest use, I boiled and ironed them, to kill any bacteria. My in-laws came over and tried to lend a hand, but I wouldn't let anyone really help. Like many overwrought new mothers, I was afraid that if I was away from him for any length of time, something bad could happen. I became a complete convert to the world of the unexpected, thinking that all of life was chaotic.

My own parents had died suddenly. First my father when I was six, when they gave him the wrong kind of blood in the hospital after a nose hemorrhage. He was thirty-three and left nine children, aged one to thirteen. My widowed mother began to drink. She died ten years later, of a broken heart as much as alcoholism. By then, we had been placed in St. Agatha Home for Children. But none of these events were nearly as heartbreaking as my longing to help my baby, and being unable to. As I write these words, thirty-two years later, the tears of helplessness stream down my cheeks as I relive those days.

My son outgrew his colic after five long, long months, and had to take allergy medicine and shots most of his young life. He had a chronic wheeze and every photo of him until he was four shows eczema on his face. But, he grew and thrived despite all of it, particularly when after we moved to San Diego in 1977. The absence of the cold dry area made his breathing easier, though he reacted to tumbleweeds and other new local allergens.

Today, he has oversized lungs so that when he has an x-ray, the technician has to take two to fit them on film. But, he's six feet tall, handsome and robust, and never took up smoking.

When Dan announced he wanted to go into the Navy after college, and become a pilot, I worried that he would not qualify, because of his allergies and his lungs. Thankfully, I was wrong. He started flying jets, then switched to Helicopters. He became a trainer, teaching young pilots, then the other trainers. Lieutenant Dan is now an Airboss (like air traffic control) on a brand new ship.

If I had my whole life to live over, and could change only one thing, I would quit smoking before becoming pregnant, or, better yet, never would have started. As a postscript, I wrote a book about my life at St. Agatha Home where we were sent to live. It opened in 1884 and has been in continuous operation ever since. The book is called *Home Kids, the Story of St. Agatha Home for Children.* All profits from the sale of the book are donated to the children of St. Agatha Home Services.

—Nancy Canfield, Speaker, Author, www.StAgathaHome.org

A Warning to Mothers

One can look back, never go back,
While traveling down Life's way.
One can tell, but not perform,
Changes in a long-past day.
This is Life, we must learn,
What we do today, tomorrow will be done.
The time spent with our children
And the words that we say,
Will they bring sweet memories
Or sad regrets someday?
This is Life, help us learn,
What we do today, tomorrow will be done.
Today, make sure to give your child
Loving words, a hug, a kiss.
Or else, tomorrow, sadly recall
The opportunities you missed.
This is Life, pray we learn,
What we do today, tomorrow will be done.

— Connie Jameson —

THE MAGIC OF MOTHERHOOD

I am known to have said, "The magic of motherhood is not for me."
For a long time this thought haunted me. Motherhood didn't come
easy to me. It took me ten years to have my son. My husband and I
battled infertility for that long!! When at times he'd wonder "a million
sperms, can't fertilize one egg?!" I'd say "that's because they don't
ask for directions either".

We had seen doctors from all over the world. An American friend
whom I had not met then but who is a sister to me now invited me
to meet with a Doctor who was a specialist in the field. And that led
to our journey to the United States.

We spent several thousands of dollars on fertility treatments.
Those were my most anxious, hopeful and saddest times. Every
cycle of treatment renewed hope, to be lost again. I remember the
many times I would crouch on the floor tugging at my tummy and
hoping for a miracle. I looked at pregnant mothers and longed to
carry that baby in me. Longed to hold that baby, longed to nourish
that baby, long to look into my husband's face and share the joy of
our child. But that moment never came.

I am an optimist. I saw the opportunity in the adversity. I was determined to use my energy and drive from the baby to the books. I
enrolled at a local University to do my Masters. We missed our baby,
but we loved other babies more. We wanted to care for our baby but
we cared for other babies. We wanted to hold our baby, but we held
other babies more. We continued to believe in God, we continued to
believe in miracles.

I finished two years of graduate studies,and was graduating in
December, but around November that year, I was sick... I was tired,
I had no appetite. My friends said perhaps I was pregnant. I said to
them, "Me? Getting pregnant would be like the sun setting in the
East!" My husband implored, that just in case I was pregnant , I
needed to take care of the baby, the baby needed nourishment!
So I went to the doctor for his sake, I literally shook the nurse
when she said I was pregnant! I went home and called her again.
I changed my walk, I changed the way I sat, I changed everything...
I wanted to protect the baby...

I was in disbelief. I was in denial. I was delighted. To be honored this
way. We thanked God day and night. Perhaps we did something right
to be blessed this way.

Our son was born, May 23rd; He shares my father's birthday.
My father never saw him, but I know he is somewhere in the
comfort of the Lord knowing we are happy and blessed. Knowing
what it means to us to have this joy in our lives. I am grateful to my
son for honoring me and giving me the title of "Mama."

Today, my son stands for love and joy in this world. I look at every
child out there and think it is mine I pray to God thanking for the joy
I may never have known if not for his grace and blessings on us.

Every mother's child is precious. And when I see how needlessly
lives are thrashed, lives are lost in the name of freedom and religion,
I weep. I weep for those mothers I share their pain. I bow humbly to
them because I cannot help them. I pray for them who are powerless
that their pain will pass.

Today, I am committed to teaching my son love and service. I want
him to grow up being a kind, humble and tolerant person. I teach
him simple lessons. What I love most is the lesson we call "The Map."
I have a huge picture of the world map in his room. We learn about
different people, cultures, countries, their location. I want him to
know and connect with people who are different from him. I
believe that if we get together as people, we can unite the world.
Governments alone can't bring about peace, we need people. People
need to contact and connect. Love, compassion, understanding,
respect are lessons we need to teach our children from very early
days. Because I believe that the true disruption and discord in lives
begins in our homes.

My father, who had a phenomenal influence in my life, taught me
from a very early age that one had to be kind especially when there
was no need. He would say that if we could unite in death, we had
to find a way to unite in life.

Often times we put our plans ahead of God's. We must learn to wait.
I was able to complete my Masters and then have my son as well.
We must remember that God has better plans for us. He sees the
whole picture. I can see how I am able to pursue my passion through
my son as my father may have seen it through me.

—Soraya Deen, Speaker, Writer, Lawyer, www.cures4conflict.com

Editor's note: There was a double miracle in her life when she and
her husband were later blessed with yet another child.

MOTHERHOOD 101–What a Curriculum!

Before you read this article find a piece of paper and a pen and copy this sentence:

Cecilia Corcoran chose to chomp chocolate while she climbed onto the carousel next to Carol Cavanaugh.

Once done, put the paper aside and read on.

Motherhood. Hm-m-m-m-m It's a lifestyle I know well. Having given birth to and reared eight children, I'm convinced God designed this profession as a surefire method of keeping us moms from becoming smug. I don't know about you, but it certainly worked in my case.

I continue to learn, through time and experience, that not only am I a teacher for my children, but my children are here to teach me. The most valuable lesson they have taught me is that how we feel about someone has nothing (nothing) to do with that person; it has everything to do with our attitude toward them. Our feelings about our mothers fall in the same category for they are shaped from our expectations of who we feel she "should" be and our disappointment that she is not. It has nothing to do with her; it has everything to do with how we'd like her to be. In other words, it has everything to do with our expectations of her, which can be changed. Once this truth really sunk in, I started to laugh. Here's why:

When at a funeral, it's customary for those who knew the deceased to get up and say a few words about her. When my body is in that box and my children stand up one at a time and tell who I was for them, I can picture the guests frowning with puzzled looks on their faces, turning to one another and whispering, "Oh my word! They all had a different mother!" Why? Because each of my children sees me quite differently. To one, I am an outstanding human being; to another, I am not; to yet another, I have been a great help getting her through troubled times; and yet another would say I was not there for her. Truth be known, I do the best I can, given who I am – just as you do and just as your mother did.

What my children feel about me has nothing (nothing) to do with who I am; it has everything to do with who they see me to be. Once you get–and I mean GET– that piece and understanding floods your mind and heart, you may be filled with a feeling as close to liberation as it gets!

NOW – If you really want to clean up attitudes you hold about YOUR mother, as you continue reading put the sentence you wrote earlier next to the rest of this article and read on. Remember – This is not about changing HER (not your job); it's about changing how you see her.

As a professional alphabetician, I focus on the letters of the alphabet as tools for personal transformation, for each letter reflects a mental attitude. The letter Cc represents our willingness to be vulnerable and free from judgment of ourselves and others– particularly women authority figures in our lives – which, of course, echoes back to Mom. What do your Cc 's look like?

As innocuous as this simple letter appears, it is one of the most difficult for women to tidy up. Any hook, loop, twist, or curl–any decoration at all in this letter–is a holding place for negative judgments about the mother figure in our lives, and it is only this judgment that keeps us negatively connected to her. Keep your Cc completely open, allowing nothing to close it off in the slightest. Draw it as a plain, unadorned 3/4 circle: clear, inviting, and free. Don't be fooled. It may look like a simple form to write, but once you begin practicing it may you find otherwise. Pick up your pen and see.

The way we write is a graphic reflection of the way we think, for the mind controls the pen. When our life changes, so does our handwriting; when we alter our handwriting patterns, our view of life and everyone in it changes. That's what therapy is all about; that's what personal transformation is all about; that's what altering handwriting patterns is all about. This is not about belief; it is about experience; I invite you to clean up your Cc and find out for yourself. Who knows, after consistent practice each day, the next time you see your mother you may, with a twinkle in your eye, arms outstretched like the letter Cc, and with all sincerity and warmth, walk up and give her a great big hug! Happy Mother's Day!

—Vimala Rodgers, PhD, Author *Your Handwriting Can Change Your Life*
www.iihs.com

Mom's Pink Robe

My Mom lived in her pink, velour robe that summer. Her bones protruded through the fabric and the bottom hem dangled threadbare. She had no reason to dress.

Leaned against a pile of pillows, Mom opened her mouth to speak but only drool leaked out. Her scrunched face cried of an anguish I could not comprehend. I reached over to clasp her trembling hands. She tried to hold mine, then she let go. She gazed into my eyes with a long, somber look. Then her brown eyes grew wider. I imagined her saying, "The cancer may be what you see out here but I'm still in here, Suzan."

I took Mom outside each morning so she could feel the ground under her and the sunshine on her. She'd been the kind of person who could walk 20 miles without pausing. Now we spent much of the afternoon getting down the block. Each time she reached the end of the street, she flashed me a slight freckled dimple.

On Mom's fifty-first birthday my brother, John, and I surprised her with a beach get-away. We arranged for a nurse to be with us the entire time. With her pink robe dangling around her tender frame and both arms around our necks, we guided her onto a beach chair. For hours she moved her toes slightly back and forth smoothing out the toasty sand. She stared toward the rolling waves along the Gulf Shore with her mouth ajar and hands in prayer atop her velour fabric.

Mom grew up on the Mississippi Gulf Coast. She'd told us that throughout her youth the beach soothed away every hurt. We hoped this visit would bring a respite from her pain. As she slumped into the cushiony beach chair, her robe swayed slightly in the breeze. I noticed tears gliding down her cheeks.

At night connected to morphine, her only other comfort seemed to be in the velour fabric of her pink robe. Mom lay still yet stirred whenever she heard our voices. She'd strain to open her eyes and listen. Mom had a perpetual look of, "I don't want to go."

Toward the end of summer we gathered her closest friends, family and clergy around her, read Bible verses and prayed over her. Her delicate frame within the pink robe showed a slight, erratic heartbeat. "Mom it is okay to let go," said John holding her right hand. "Please go with God," said her daughter, Adele, brushing her hands along Mom's temples. "Be at peace. I love you, Mom," I whispered with my hand pressed upon her heart. I then felt her stillness and watched her intently as tears streamed down. I didn't want to miss a moment of our final memory.

Mom's eyes looked as if she'd seen the dead and I imagined that she may have. I envisioned her Father with his generous grin beckoning her forth with sweeping hand gestures. A sigh labored from her quivering mouth. Her eyes rolled back and her body became limp. My body heaved as I gasped for air. In my head I knew she'd left her pain. In my heart I knew that in spite of everything, I wasn't ready to say goodbye. Who ever is? Two men from the morgue arrived with the gurney. They placed Mom on it with slow precision - in her pink, velour robe. We gathered around to embrace her one last time. Yet who was this 80 pound brittle woman? Her cancer left us with nothing to hug. I clung to Mom and her pink robe. I heard someone mutter, "Come on honey, let go." I couldn't. I followed the men as they wheeled her out of the house. Walking along side them, I bawled over her slight frame down the driveway. Before they placed her into the Hearst, I reached down to feel the softness once again of the velour robe. I rubbed my hand along the length of it. I then hugged Mom's placid body one last time as my own body collapsed around hers in uncontrollable heaves.

I felt my body being lifted, as if by a crane, off of my Mother and her robe. "Okay young lady. We must go now," one said. The men loaded her into the back of the Hearst. I watched them drive away en route to the crematory. I sank down on the hard cement driveway and curled to my side. My best friend is gone-forever, I realized. What had been unsaid? I contemplated. With this I rolled over and sprawled against the lawn.

I reached over and grabbed some clumps of grass from the lawn. Then I pounded my fists over and over into the spongy turf. I wondered if I'd ever get through the numbing pain. Will I ever get over losing my Mom? I pondered.

I leaned into the grass and rubbed my hands along the blades. My throat felt parched. I began to choke as I grappled for air. I sat up and wiped my wet face with the front of my shirt. The blades of grass were not as soft as Mom's pink robe. I longed to feel it once again.

—Suzan Tusson-McNeil, Sherpa, Coach, Artist
©2006 All Rights Reserved, www.wisdomquestcoaching.com
Received Honorable Mention for Memoirs/Personal Essays
Writer's Digest Contest

Motherhood

Mother: The most beautiful word on the lips of mankind.
—Kahlil Gibran

For one who has awakened to true motherhood, every creature
is his or her child. Such love, such Motherhood, is Divine Love,
which is God.
—Amma (Mother), Mata Amritanandamayi, India
Messages from Amma: In the Language of the Heart, www.amma.org

Mothers are fonder than fathers of their children because they are
more certain they are their own.
—Aristotle

If a woman has to choose between catching a fly ball and saving
an infant's life, she will choose to save the infant's life without
even considering if there are men on base.
—Dave Barry

The mother's heart is the child's schoolroom.
—Henry Ward Beecher

If evolution really works, how come mothers only have two hands?
—Milton Berle

No one who traces the history of motherhood, of the home,
of child-rearing practices will ever assume the eternal permanence
of our own way of institutionalizing them.
—Jessie Bernard

Women know the way to rear up children (to be just).
They know a simple, merry, tender knack of tying sashes,
fitting baby-shoes, and stringing pretty words that make no sense.
And kissing full sense into empty words.
—Elizabeth Barrett Browning

Some are kissing mothers and some are scolding mothers,
but it is love just the same, and most mothers kiss and scold together.
—Pearl S. Buck, Author, Nobel Prize for Literature, 1938

A mother's love for her child is like nothing else in the world.
It knows no law, no pity, it dares all things and crushes down
remorselessly all that stands in its path.
—Agatha Christie

There is a point where you aren't as much mom and daughter
as you are adults and friends. It doesn't happen for everyone—
but it did for Mom and me.
—Jamie Lee Curtis, celebrity daughter of Janet Leigh and Tony Curtis

A suburban mother's role is to deliver children obstetrically once,
and by car forever after.
—Peter De Vries

I wear my heart on my sleeve.
—Diana, Princess of Wales

My mother is a walking miracle...
—Leonardo DiCaprio, Actor

My mother is a poem I'll never be able to write,
though everything I write is a poem to my mother.
—Sharon Doubiago

Life began with waking up and loving my mother's face.
—George Eliot

Men are what their mothers made them.
—Ralph Waldo Emerson

When I stopped seeing my mother with the eyes of a child,
I saw the woman who helped me give birth to myself.
—Nancy Friday

The love of a parent for a child is the love
that should grow towards separation.
— Kahlil Gibran

It's not easy being a mother. If it were easy, fathers would do it.
—From the TV Series *The Golden Girls*

Becoming a mother makes you the mother of all children.
From now on each wounded, abandoned, frightened child is yours.
You live in the suffering mothers of every race and creed and weep
with them. You long to comfort all who are desolate.
—Charlotte Gray

Women do not have to sacrifice personhood if they are mothers.
They do not have to sacrifice motherhood in order to be persons.
Liberation was meant to expand women's opportunities, not to limit
them. The self-esteem that has been found in new pursuits can also
be found in mothering.
—Elaine Heffner

God could not be everywhere, so he created mothers.
—Jewish Proverb

The real religion of the world comes from women much more than
from men — from mothers most of all, who carry the key of our souls
in their bosoms.
—Oliver Wendell Holmes

A mother is the truest friend we have, when trials heavy and sudden,
fall upon us; when adversity takes the place of prosperity; when
friends who rejoice with us in our sunshine desert us; when trouble
thickens around us, still will she cling to us, and endeavor by her kind
precepts and counsels to dissipate the clouds of darkness, and cause
peace to return to our hearts.
—Washington Irving

Now, as always, the most automated appliance in a household
is the mother.
—Beverly Jones

A mother is a person who seeing there are only four pieces of pie for five people, promptly announces she never did care for pie.
—Tenneva Jordan

Motherhood brings as much joy as ever, but it still brings boredom, exhaustion, and sorrow too. Nothing else ever will make you as happy or as sad, as proud or as tired, for nothing is quite as hard as helping a person develop his own individuality especially while you struggle to keep your own.
—Marguerite Kelly and Elia Parsons

I never knew what how much joy it was to give up and sacrifice things until I had children.
—Sandy Liarakos, mother of all sons

All that I am or ever hope to be, I owe to my angel Mother.
—Abraham Lincoln

When you are a mother, you are never really alone in your thoughts. A mother always has to think twice, once for herself and once for her child.
—Sophia Loren, *Women and Beauty*

That best academy, a mother's knee.
—James Russell Lowell

When a child is born, God sprinkles a bit of magic into the heart of the mother. As this precious little miracle is laid upon the mother's breast, this magic brings feelings of unparalleled love and incredible awe... and her heart will never be the same.
—Adria Manary, Speaker, Author of *More Mommy Magic – 506 Ways To Nurture Your Child*, www.mommymagic.com

Few misfortunes can befall a boy which brings worse consequences than to have a really affectionate mother.
—W. Somerset Maugham

When momma's not happy – no one's happy!
—Dr. Phil McGraw, Author, Life and Relationship Coach

Women's Liberation is just a lot of foolishness.
It's the men who are discriminated against. They can't bear children.
And no one's likely to do anything about that.
—Golda Meir

At work, you think of the children you have left at home.
At home, you think of the work you've left unfinished.
Such a struggle is unleashed within yourself.
Your heart is rent.
—Golda Meir

Anyone who doesn't miss the past never had a mother.
—Gregory Nunn

Her children arise up, and call her blessed.
—Proverbs 31:28

The moment a child is born, the mother is also born.
She never existed before. The woman existed, but the mother, never.
A mother is something absolutely new.
—Rajneesh

Women's rights in essence is really a movement for freedom,
a movement for equality, for the dignity of all women, for those
who work outside the home and those who dedicate themselves
with more altruism than any profession I know to being wives and
mothers, cooks and chauffeurs, and child psychologists and loving
human beings.
—Jill Ruckelshaus

An ounce of mother is worth a pound of priests.
—Spanish Proverb

The phrase "working mother" is redundant.
—Jane Sellman

Motherhood has a very humanizing effect.
Everything gets reduced to essentials.
—Meryl Streep, Actress

Who is best taught? He who has first learned from his mother.
—*The Talmud*

Mother is the name for God in the lips and hearts of little children.
—William Makepeace Thackeray, English novelist

Mothers are the sacred vessels from which life overflows.
—Catherine Tilley

Mothers are the bearers of life, the caretakers of our children, the light of our future.
—Catherine Tilley

A Freudian slip is when you say one thing but mean your mother.
—Unknown

Being a full-time mother is one of the highest salaried jobs...
since the payment is pure love.
—Mildred B. Vermont

My mother was the most beautiful woman I ever saw.
All I am I owe to my mother. I attribute all my success in life to the moral, intellectual and physical education I received from her.
—George Washington, First President of the United States

Motherhood is neither a duty nor a privilege, but simply the way that humanity can satisfy the desire for physical immortality and triumph over the fear of death.
—Rebecca West

Most of all the other beautiful things in life come by twos and threes by dozens and hundreds. Plenty of roses, stars, sunsets, rainbows, brothers, and sisters, aunts and cousins, but only one mother in the whole world.
— Kate Douglas Wiggin

Of all the rights of women, the greatest is to be a mother.
—Lin Yutang

SO, HOW IS YOUR DAY?

As a mother of 3, one being a baby, I really wish I had time to think of a good, smart, funny, heartfelt thing to write. But reality is that I was awoken at 5 to nurse my baby girl, the boys were in my bed jumping around and fighting by 5:30 and my husband who just returned late last night at midnight from traveling rolled out of bed to avoid the disturbance and headed for the shower. By 6:15 we were eating breakfast–and that is a circus in itself since no one likes the same things and getting the 5 year old to sit for more than 10 seconds is a challenge.

Baby crying for her cereal, braces hurt on the 7-year-old (since when did they put braces on kids so early), get the snacks in the backpacks, homework done, medicines and vitamins into each kid, laundry into the dryer, pick up things as walk through the house, shoes on kids, hair combed (keeping spray gel and a comb in the car is great for boys), brushing my own hair is optional - feeling lucky to get sweats on that actually match, holding baby all the while... Even once the kids are in school there is so much to do - always shopping, cleaning, feeding or playing with or changing the baby. Never a dull moment. I know this is the reason that later there will be empty nest syndrome, but that doesn't help at the moment! It's the very small pockets of moments when I get to be with just one child that I truly enjoy their individuality.

I take a lot of photos and love to work on their albums and keepsake boxes, because those are the moments that I see how fast it is all going, and those are the things the kids can't wait to re-look at to see how much they have grown or how silly something they made me is, and how much I treasure it!

The heart of a mother is really not her own any longer - she gives it away freely to her children and her spouse. Her heart aches when anyone is sick or hurt, and covers it up when it is her own, because it never seems to matter as much when a child needs something. Always a purpose, always a need. Sometimes a busy mother has to remember that being needed and loved is a basic desire for everyone and on that scale she is filled up. Yet it will be nice to someday go to the bathroom by myself with the door closed!

—Jennifer Sedlock, Speaker, Author, Mommy of three
www.JenniferSpeaks.com

Mothering Yourself

7 Blessings for Nurturing Your Soul

Our journeys began as we basked in our mothers' protective wombs, clinging to their every breath to nourish our souls. They embraced us for the first time in their loving arms, providing protection and unconditional acceptance. We can imagine their first tears on our cheeks, hear their first laughs, and feel their soft kisses. As we appreciate our mothers for giving us our lives, we can also honor them as role models for nurturing ourselves.

Take a moment to envision your mother—the woman who gave you birth and first nurtured your soul. Observe how she has nurtured herself and rejoiced in her womanhood. Do you like what you see?

Traditionally, women have been taught by the mothers of their mothers to appease others and then (if there is time) take care of themselves. That convention needs to change. Indeed, it's critical that women welcome themselves often into the nurturing experience of self-love. Why? Because it's the most vital way to honor others and the world we care for.

So how can you honor life more fully? You can carve your day around activities that can be called the **Seven Heavenly Blessings**. When you do, they will allow you to mother yourself in a loving way.

Blessing 1: Say a Morning Gratitude Prayer
Begin your day embracing yourself in silent prayer, even if you close your eyes for only five minutes. If you can't find time at the beginning of your day, take several minutes in the evening to say a prayer of gratitude. What do you give thanks for in your day? In your life?

Select a sacred space and turn your prayer into a ritual - perhaps before you get out of bed, when you are in the shower, or sitting in your favorite chair. For these precious moments, close your eyes, listen deeply to the sound of your breath, and surround yourself with beautiful images of Mother Nature–waterfalls, flowers, streams, oceans, mountains.

Visualize your family, friends, and coworkers in a circle as they surround you with love and light. Be open to receiving their kind words as you express your gratitude for them.

Blessing 2: Lavish in Your Inner Beauty
It's important to honor your physical beauty for it reflects the glorious temple you live in. Your beauty deserves your attention and appreciation. Consider these ways to nurture yourself in its reflection.

- Soak in a luxurious bath. Cleanse your beautiful body from top to toe.
- Focus on only eating nourishing foods to fuel your energy. Observe how you feel.
- At least once a month, pamper yourself with your favorite spa treatment-a manicure, a pedicure, a facial, a massage.
- Hire a color and image consultant to show you how colors can bring out the essence of your beauty. Brighten your wardrobe and coordinate it with your hair, your skin, your energy.
- If you feel sleepy, take a nap. Yes, even in the afternoon. It's okay!

When you take time for yourself-just watch. As you shift the energy within you and see how energy shifts around you, you'll look and feel more beautiful than ever.

Blessing 3: Surround Your Space with What You Love
Create a nurturing sanctuary for yourself. No matter what space constraints you may have, surround yourself with exquisite "jewels."

- Pay attention to favorite colors, pictures, fabrics, wisdom, books, music, plants, flowers, and paintings.
- Choose a soothing fabric and wrap it the chair you love to sit in. Buy music that inspires you.
- Select affirmation cards and let them echo your heart's divine message.
- Take a mini-vacation in your mind.

Most important of all, sink your whole being into this sacred space, for it will lovingly remind you of all things good.

Blessing 4: Follow Your Passion
Finally just do it!
Listen to your passion with wild abandon, and pursue an endeavor or hobby that has always called to you. Leave out the deadlines and let your inclinations lead your actions.

A few possibilities:
- Take a trip to a special new place.
- Learn a new craft.
- Paint a daring picture.
- Begin writing a novel.
- Learn to fly an airplane.
- If it's the right time, make a career change.

You're nurturing yourself when you can tune into the electrifying energy of being alive, when you can muster the courage to move beyond your fears-just one step starts it.

Blessing 5: Create a Vision of Your Future Now
Taking care of yourself now means paying attention to what you want in the future. Try these ideas:
- Find photos in magazines of places and activities that you desire, then create a collage and post it where you can see it often.
- Visualize your ideal day, week, month, or year.
  Exactly how are you spending your precious time?
- Imagine yourself five years from now. Where are you?
  How did you get there?
  Who is with you?
  What journeys did you experience along the way?

Stating your intention of what you desire applies to every word you write or say, every expression you make, every action you take, and every thought you have. If you focus on always creating a beautiful life canvas of your future, you can actually feel the outcomes today.

Blessing 6: Build Your Support Team
People can only achieve greatness by surrounding themselves with those they love and admire. This should not be an effort, only a natural expression of life. How can you surround yourself with role models who lead you into the future and team members who support your journey? A few suggestions:
- Belong to a mastermind group.
- Create relationships with mentors to advise you on your career.
- Identify the true friends you know you can lean on.
- Get to know the wonderful people in your inner and outer circles.

Although people in your circles will be different as you change and grow, you're wise to continually build your support teams.

Blessing 7: Surrender to Life in Your Spiritual Sanctuary
As you feel nurtured in all aspects of yourself, you know where your spark originated-from your spiritual core. Keep exploring deeper into the sanctuary of your own spirituality and you'll find a deep well of mothering. Whether you attend a temple, a church, a mosque-or if you pray or meditate or go on pilgrimages-know you have a Source to rely on in your spiritual sanctuary.

Today. Right now. Decide how you will imbue yourself with a mother's nurturing care so the flowers of your life will grow stronger and more colorful around you.

—Lisa R. Delman, Speaker, Author of *Dear Mom, I've Always Wanted You to Know... Daughters Share Letters from the Heart*, Penguin 2005. Founder and visionary of the international Heart Project. Encourages women to articulate their emotions sacredly on paper initiating a journey that often leads to self-discovery, healing past wounds, and an opportunity to feel liberated. www.TheHeartProject.com

Mother Within

Our Most Treasured Mother... The Mother Within

We all know about Beaver and Wally's picture perfect home life with the quintessential Mom, June Clever, on the TV sit-com, Leave it to Beaver, who always had the cookies and milk waiting for her boys when they came home from school. We also know about the now-legendary tale of the domestic horror relationship of abuse, alcoholism and insanity between Hollywood superstar, Joan Crawford and her adopted daughter Christina as revealed in the movie Mommie Dearest. Luckily, for most of us, our relationship with our Mother was not that of June or Joan, but probably somewhere in between these extremes.

Because the dynamics of relationships with our Mothers can be very challenging, we often feel fearful of never receiving the nurturing and inner peace we all yearn for.

I know something about being afraid. As a child I grew up in an atmosphere of fear. Although my Mother did her best to nurture me amidst the chaos of a dysfunctional home, there remained a void within me. Being the fifth of six children, my Mom was extremely busy keeping the household running with little time to spend with yet another newborn... me.

Knowing she was giving all she had to give, I found no use in blaming her for the way our family dynamics had unfolded, but one challenge remained... I still yearned for more nurturing. Then one day I made a remarkable discovery that changed my life forever. I discovered I could be my own Mother and get all the nurturing I needed at any time, day or night and diminish the fear. The Mother I found was not an external mother, but my own Mother Within.

Quietly deep within each one of us lies a loving nurturing aspect of self, which resides in the heart. Unfortunately many of us don't seem to be able to locate this elusive heart.

If you think of your mind as your ego, consider this loving aspect within the Heart of self as another level of consciousness; when you go into this place you tap into a more kind, gentle and nurturing inner voice beyond anything you have ever experienced in the outer world, the voice of the Mother Within. Between Head and Heart there is a division; sometimes it's almost a civil war. For most people the Head dominates our relationships; it likes to be in control and makes us doubt anything outside of its domain. The nurturing Heart is the place beyond the physical, where the five senses are trumped by something greater.

Many people balk at the idea of listening to something other than their head. We are taught to use our logical mind, and anything other than reason is usually discounted or scoffed at. People can much more easily accept being in the head as opposed to being in the heart. As you continue to practice this technique, you will be easily able to distinguish between my ego and my Mother Within. Anyone can make this connection, as you are only a few steps away from reaching this place.

Inside my sanctuary I relax and do breathing exercises before moving my attention from head to heart. Once in that place I listen, and the doorway to my Mother Within speaks to me. The message is always kind, loving and nurturing, everything I yearned for. Most of us only lead lives within our heads, and have lost the balance in our beings. The technique of getting to the Mother Within allows for a connection between head and heart that is otherwise missing, and offers the nurturing often missing from everyday life. When you connect with your heart, fear and doubt vanishes. By quieting the mind and going within one's self, you will be able to make a tangible connection to your nurturing self.

In matters where you are unsure, The Mother Within takes the un-certainty out of decisions. If you are fearful or need more nurturing, it allows a perspective that brings a peace that was missing. Anyone searching for revelations on self, or situations, can greatly benefit from practicing this technique. Don't be surprised, though, if you receive unexpected answers. Your heart knows things that your mind doesn't, or that your ego tries to guise. Because I have practiced my connection with my Mother Within countless times, and used it as a guide in my life, I am able to proceed without doubt.

So when you yearn for more nurturing, find a comfortable place where you will be totally uninterrupted for at least 10 to 15 minutes. Sit with your spine straight. Once you are comfortable, take a few deep breaths, and then slowly close your eyes. When you are fully relaxed, slowly breathe in through your nose and out through your mouth.

With each breath gently move all of your attention from your head to your heart. If it helps, visualize a feather falling through the air. Make the process that effortless. Start breathing fully into the heart.

As you move into the heart, you will become aware of the continuous flow of thoughts that go on inside of you. This "noise" can be overwhelming at first. Try to place yourself in a place above the noise and do your best to just listen and observe.

It is not hard to connect with your Heart, and it becomes obvious when that occurs. The chatter of the mind will fade away and the superhighway of thoughts disappear into the background and are replaced by a sense of peace and freedom. With this connection you will experience tranquility, and a feeling of love as you have accessed your Mother Within.

Being in this peaceful place brings about a quiet revolution. The past relationship with your external Mother will no longer be the arbiter of your life. Here, being in your Heart, you will find a doorway to a kinder gentler inner voice more nurturing than that which comes from your mind or any external person. In this serene spot you will be able to connect with your Mother Within.

Because you are now in the Heart you will able to connect with the voice of your Mother Within. The only thing you need do is to listen. From this wellspring emerges a nurturing that is greater than your own; a nurturing that is in all of us, but one that mostly goes untapped. From this state of grace your way will become clear and you will hear the loving messages of your Mother Within.

When you are ready, slowly open your eyes and move your body gently from side to side. As you become aware of your surroundings you will feel loved, refreshed, at peace, and inspired to go about your day appreciating the joy of life.

As you do this process on a regular basis, your new life can be likened to the mythological story of the Phoenix Rising. This mythological bird in Egyptian mythology consumed itself by fire and then rose renewed from its ashes. If your relationship with your Mother feels as if it is in ruins, be confident that you can rise again by connecting within as you create a new loving relationship within your self that will be exhilarating and enlightening. So follow your heart, connect with your Mother Within and go forth in peace.

—Gloria Boileau, Speaker, Author of the book, *STOP THE FEAR! - Finding Peace In A Chaotic World*. Gloria offers solutions for creating a more enriched and complete life than you ever could have imagined. Gloria@GloriaBoileau.com

Mothers

Beauty isn't just skin deep; beauty is womb deep.
—Mary Marcdante, Speaker, Author *My Mother, My Friend*
www.MaryMarcdante.com

What if you chose your mother?
Out of all the mothers there were to chose from,
what if you selected her because some how you knew
that she was the who would be your greatest ally
and your catalyst for achieving your greatest human potential?

—Catherine Tilley

I REMEMBER MY MOTHER

She never sat straight upon a chair.
Three-quarters of her hung in the air,
Ready to jump up to do or to cook
Whatever I might overlook.

From New York to Detroit she drove alone.
No turnpikes then and no cell phone.
Just two little girls alone in the car,
Certain she could follow map or star.

And though we didn't always get along,
I remember how she could play any song,
And I expect to hear those tunes again,
When next we meet, just 'round the bend.

—Rosalie Ferrer Kramer, Speaker, Poet—
Author *Dancing in the Dark:*
Things My Mother Never Told Me
www.authorsden.com/rosaliefkramer

My Mother

I've come to share a sample
Of a beautiful example,
        My Mother.

If a thing needed doing
She did it!
If we needed support
She gave it!
        My Mother.

If I needed a lesson
She taught it.
If I needed some knowledge
She found it,
        My Mother.

If I needed understanding
She understood,
If my heart got broken
She fixed it,
        My Mother.

If I got it right
She praised me.
If I made a mistake
She forgave me,
        My Mother.

If I needed a helping hand
I got hers.
If I wondered about life
She answered me,
        My Mother.

This is just a sample
Of a beautiful example,
        My Mother.

—Janice Baylis, Author of *Sex, Symbols and Dreams,* and
Sleep On It: The Practical Side of Dreaming

Dedicated to my mother, Adella Hinshaw (1899-1972)

A LOVE, MY LOVE

I laugh,
She smiles
A friend,
My playmate

I learn,
She teaches
A genius,
My almanac

I hurt,
She heals
A doctor,
My cure

I eat,
She's pleased
A chef,
My nutrition

I'm misunderstood
She understands
A psychologist,
My wisdom

I'm safe
She's strong
A hero,
My protection

I dream,
She encourages
A mentor,
My mom

—Aleka Mesaros, Age 15—

Hairy Apes, Ugly Ducklings, and Swans

A very big part of my mother's beauty to me was her laughter. Her sense of humor comforted me through many nights of tears during my growing up years. While I know there were happy moments, my memories of sixth, seventh, and eighth grade are more often filled with running from the taunts of peers, mostly boys, on the way to and from school.

I was tomboy with a big crook in my nose and feet as big as the floor tiles in the school hallway. I was flat chested and string bean tall. My arms were so hairy that when the boys saw me they'd shout at the top of their lungs, "Look, there goes the flat-chested hairy ape."

One particularly brutal day, I remember running the entire four blocks home, and bursting into tears as I opened the front door and saw my mother. After spilling my story, she told me that boys teased her the same way when she was my age. "They called me 'Four-Eyes,'" she said, "Because I wore glasses, and 'Greasy Grace' because my thin hair laid so flat on my head." She said she cried just like me, but her mother taught her to laugh it off. She promised me that one day I'd "blossom," the hair on my arms would fade away, and that even though I felt like the ugly duckling, someday I would look in the mirror and see a beautiful swan.

Her words wrapped around me like a hug. I repeated her promise like a chanting Buddhist as I grew by an inch or two every summer, reaching my final height of five feet ten inches in my early twenties. By then, my feet had grown to a size ten and continue to expand – size twelve as I write. As I've grown older, the hair on my arms has faded away just like Mom said. The only thing that's blossomed though, is the rose bush on my balcony. It's hard not to notice cleavage on the beach, but for me the health issues outweigh any satisfaction I'd gain from artificially blooming my breasts.

Some days I look in the mirror and catch a glimpse of a swan, and some days I hear a lot of quacking. I've learned to smile; I hear my mother: "Look at that beautiful long neck."

—Mary Marcdante, Speaker, Author My Mother, My Friend
www.MaryMarcdante.com

Reprinted with permission from Simon & Schuster.

MAMA MUSE

It's great to think back on how my mother and I have grown closer through the years. When I was little, I adored her. She was like God to me. I used to dream about the two of us being roommates when I went to college. Oh, how much fun we would have together! Then when I was in about 4th-5th grade I went through the stage when I was "too cool" to be mommy's darling. If she ever tried to hug me or kiss me I acted like, "Oh, yuck, get away!" Throughout my teenage years, she and I became very close again. What a brat I had been for acting mean in my "tweens." No matter how naughty I was, Mom never stopped caring for me. She was unconditional in her love for me.

We began our "mudder-dotter" adventures when I was three. I named it that when I was little because I couldn't pronounce "mother-daughter" and the name stuck as we made dates to do girlie girl things... manicures, facials, massages, tea parties. What we were really doing was bonding. My mother has one of the friendliest, most outgoing personalities there is. She treats others exactly how she wants them to treat her and she always sees the best in people. She believes in helping others live their dreams as she has helped me live mine. I can still hear her voice as she encourages me when I am frightened: "You can do it, you can do it, you're the greatest!"

What I've learned from my mother is to be real and authentic and to love grandly. Life is about communication and understanding. She is always telling me "you don't stop laughing because you grow old, you grow old because you stop laughing!" We laugh a lot.

My mom and I have a mother-daughter bond that will never be broken. She is my "Mama Muse," an inspiration and a motivation to me and others, although she'll tell you she is just "Mom Amuse." I want to follow in her footsteps by being the star she's taught me to be. Today we call ourselves the "Dynamic Duo." We are hosting TV and radio shows together, we write together, we speak together, and yes, we do have a house at college together.
I can't imagine a greater love.

—Heather Brittany, Actress on the TV series, *Veronica Mars*

Editor's Note:
Together, Heather and her mother, Cynthia Brian, write a column called *Tea for Two-A Mother/Daughter Brew* as well as host a popular radio program on World Talk Radio. www.star-style.com

A TRIBUTE TO MOM

As I think back over the years when I was a kid,
It amazes me how Mom managed to do as much as she did.
Of course, she was the first one up and the last one to bed.
But even so, back in the 30s, life on the farm wasn't easy you know.
She sure had a lot of get up and go.
I remember that old washing machine,
with just a foot pedal and a push lever, she kept our clothes clean.
Not to mention the old wooden churn, with a crank and a creak
she made butter, about once a week.
With socks to darn and clothes to mend, work piled up, there was no end.
When spring came around there was a garden to plant and all summer to
tend. And when baby chicks arrived, the brooder house needed scrubbing
and the stove put back in. Canning time was really a chore.
Fruits and vegetables stacked high on the kitchen floor.
When Dad butchered, there was meat to cut and hams to cure,
Then lard to render, that was for sure.
Milking cows by hand was a daily routine,
like gathering eggs and separating milk from the cream.
The calves and pigs would get the skim,
with all these chores, she stayed pretty trim.
In summer time on many a hot day,
She pitched right in to help with the hay.
When shocking grain you could depend,
She'd keep up with the best of them.
In the fall of the year there was corn to pick,
T'would have made the average woman just sick.
For 5 or 6 weeks from day till dark,
had to throw like the dickens before the snow starts.
In winter time when roads were blocked and schools were closed,
she knitted us warm mittens so we never froze.
With the snow to shovel and water to carry, she chopped wood too,
when necessary.
On Saturday night we'd all get a bath,
we'd forget about school and all that math.
With hot water from the stove's reservoir
we could hardly wait to see a movie starring Dorothy Lamour.
But Mom had produce to sell and groceries to buy,
Lord knows she had little time to sit down and cry.
She just took things in stride, one day at a time.
And never seemed to tire when in her prime.
Yes, these are just a few of the thing my momma did,
and still found time to love all seven kids.

—Your son Vernon

Editor's note: Vernon Lundquist, Country Singer and the eldest of the 7 Iowa
farm kids. Written about and for his mother Nellie Reimers Lundquist,
beloved grandmother of Sheryl Roush, editor of this publication.

SWEET SENTIMENTS

My mother's actual maiden name is Fudge. Yes, I know, "isn't that sweet?" For years I have wanted to do something for her with her maiden name in mind. This year I finally did it. I found a custom chocolate manufacturer and a good artist and we created a product known as "Laura Elizabeth Fudge" Premium Confections.

Using my mom's signature we created the label design and "corporate" slogan: "You deserve a Special Treat!" Then I wrote a legend for the back of the label. The legend was written as if this were a real retail product created by a real company known as "Laura Elizabeth Fudge." I then signed it with the names of the "employees" (names of her parents, siblings, husband, son and daughter-in-law).

We produced two boxes of chocolate bars, milk and dark. Then we created a box of truffles and another of almond nut cups. I shipped several boxes to mom with a descriptive letter and she cried joys of happiness for days! When I called her she choked up again.

As a memento I had the label art and legend printed on an 8 x 10" sheet and framed it for her. Here is what the legend said:

Beginning on October 5, 1919 Laura Elizabeth Fudge made the world a sweeter place. A defining characteristic of our founder, Laura Elizabeth Fudge, is her wholesome spirit. The cheerful attitude of genuinely wanting to provide others with a "special treat" is at the core of all LEF products. Whether it is through a personal gift, a nurturing gesture, a willing shoulder or a thoughtful act of generosity, the spirit of Laura Elizabeth Fudge is service to others. We hope that you pick up this spirit with each sweet bite. You can rest assured that the loving touch has gone into every step of the process of creating these "special treats."

LEF was "founded" in Rochelle, Louisiana and soon expanded to Winfield, then to Little Rock, Arkansas. During the years of World War II operations were moved to the San Francisco Bay area and later relocated to Little Rock.

Share the joy, savor the sweet taste, feel the warmth and caring of Laura Elizabeth Fudge.

Sincerely,
James, Rhoda, Lizzie, Harvey, Elizabeth, Ed, Earl, Jim, Kathy and Paula Sue

—Jim Cathcart, Speaker, Author

MOTHERS IN PRISON

Toastmasters International offers a special, not-for-profit Gavel Club program for those in correctional facilities to improve their listening, thinking and speaking skills. This enables those released to ease back into society with greater confidence and higher morals.

I work with inmates within the California Department of Corrections with three groups of women and two groups of men. Each of these groups has approximately 20 members, ideal for practicing better communication and leadership skills.

Stereotypes may drive us to think of these people as inhuman (many people must as their actions show); however, I find that they are just like you and me. Most of the women that I work with are mothers who have been separated from their children for years. The separation is physical; however, these women have a great bond with their children.

When one of the women gives a speech telling about the success of their child or children, everyone shares in the joy.

When someone is suffering due to problems that their children are experiencing, all of the women come to provide comfort and aid to the mother who is suffering. There are many times that I have seen everyone in the group cry over the problems that the children of one of the members of their group was having.

One night, one of the women told of her two-year-old grandson dying. She shared that her prison mate said her actions were the reason God took her grandson. That night I witnessed all of the women in the group, irrespective of what their crimes had been–murder, robbery, etc.,–break down and cry and gathered around the grandmother to support her.

The bond that these women have with their children and grand-children is what gives them the courage to go on. They want to rehabilitate so they can get out to rejoin their family and provide some guidance to their children.

—Darrell Zeller

I'm Sorry Mom!

I'm sorry for the troubles, and the worries I brought you.
I'm sorry for my mistakes, I didn't mean to make you blue.
When I was young and growing up, Living in your home for so long,
I made many people sad, I did many things wrong.
So I thought that I could show you now,
By moving away and being on my own,
That I was finally straightened out,
I wanted to prove to you I am finally maturely grown.
But I haven't done to well at that, I guess it goes to show,
You never really solved it all, You never really know.
I'd like to show you now, I need to take the time to say,
Thanks for accepting both the good and bad,
I hope you have a Wonderful Mother's Day!

© 1989 Laurie Meade
www.lauriemeade.com

HAPPY MOTHER'S DAY MOM

You're the mother of the man I married many years ago,
If tomorrow never comes for me, my feelings you should know,
I feel respect and pride for you in all that you have done,
Accept these words of gratitude from the wife of your only son.
Wisdom, strength and courage are traits I see in you,
You bless me with compassion in the things you say and do.
Our thanks is often left unsaid and I love you seldom told,
The sacrifices you've made for us my heart will always hold.
Your precious heart made of gold and feels our joy and sorrow,
The faith you have in us gives me hope in a new tomorrow.
You always stand beside us in life's trials and its tests,
Of all the gifts you've given me, your love I treasure best.
My prayer is God will bless you for your kind and caring ways,
I promise Mom to love you always each and every day.

—Judith A. Duran—
For my wonderful mother-in-law, Ruby Lovejoy

A MOTHER'S SECRET REVEALED

I would like to contribute to your book BUT I have some kind of disease. This goes all the way back to elementary school. Whenever I am asked to write something (even in my journaling) my mind, which is constantly in movement, goes completely blank. So, with that said this is my contribution. I know you will grasp the meaning a be able to put it into usable form.

As you know my daughter, Kristina, wrote the poem "Moms" which you published in your last book, "Heart of a Woman." We purchased several copies and Kris gave them as Christmas gifts to friends and family.

She sent a copy to my mom in Michigan with a note. I spoke to my mom about a month later. She told me to tell Kris "Thanks for the book. She had everyone (rest of family) read the poem when they were gathered for Christmas. She was so glad that someone else in the family has the ability to write because she always wanted to write."

I was stunned. This was something I have never known about my mom. My mother is emotionally closed off. She has never shared her dreams or desires with us. To receive this little peek into my mother's true essence is such a gift to me. I thank my beautiful daughter, my mom, and you, for giving me this gift that I will cherish forever.

—Sue Nigro, Mother of Kristina Marie Nigro

MOMS

They rule the earth in some sort of way
They try to be jolly and cheerful all day
Moms work hard to put food on the table
Whether they live in mansions,
houses or stables
Their love for you will always last
They try to find time to play with you
and have a blast
As for my mom she is kind
and always has time to spend with me
As it should be.

—Kristina Marie Nigro, Age 10—

Mother's Day

Ancient Celebrations of Mothers and Motherhood

People in many ancient cultures celebrated holidays honoring motherhood, personified as a goddess.
Here are just a few of those:

  • Ancient Greeks celebrated a holiday in honor of Rhea, the mother of the gods

  • Ancient Romans celebrated a holiday in honor of Cybele, a mother goddess, March 22-25 - the celebrations were notorious enough that followers of Cybele were banished from Rome

  • In the British Isles and Celtic Europe, the goddess Brigid, and later her successor St. Brigid, were honored with a spring Mother's Day, connected with the first milk of the ewes

Julia Ward Howe's Mother's Day for Peace

Julia Ward Howe tried to establish a Mother's Day in America
She became well-known during and after the American Civil War as the author of the words to the "Battle Hymn of the Republic," but was horrified by the carnage of the Civil War and the Franco-Prussian War.

In 1870, she tried to issue a manifesto for peace at international peace conferences in London and Paris (it was much like the later Mother's Day Peace Proclamation).

In 1872, she began promoting the idea of a "Mother's Day for Peace" to be celebrated on June 2, honoring peace, motherhood and womanhood.

In 1873, women in 18 cities in America held a Mother's Day for Peace gathering. Boston celebrated the Mother's Day for Peace for at least 10 years. The celebrations died out when Howe was no longer paying most of the cost for them, although some celebrations continued for 30 years. Howe turned her efforts to working for peace and women's rights in other ways.

A postage stamp was issued in honor of Julia Ward Howe in 1988 – without mention of Mother's Day, though.

Mother's Day Proclamation - 1870
— Julia Ward Howe —

Arise then...women of this day!
Arise, all women who have hearts!
Whether your baptism be of water or of tears!

Say firmly:
"We will not have questions answered by irrelevant agencies,
Our husbands will not come to us, reeking with carnage,
For caresses and applause.
Our sons shall not be taken from us to unlearn
All that we have been able to teach them of charity,
mercy and patience.
We, the women of one country,
Will be too tender of those of another country
To allow our sons to be trained to injure theirs."

From the voice of a devastated Earth a voice goes up with
Our own. It says: "Disarm! Disarm!
The sword of murder is not the balance of justice."
Blood does not wipe our dishonor,
Nor violence indicate possession.
As men have often forsaken the plough and the anvil
At the summons of war,
Let women now leave all that may be left of home
For a great and earnest day of counsel.

Let them meet first, as women, to bewail and
commemorate the dead.
Let them solemnly take counsel with each other as to the means
Whereby the great human family can live in peace...
Each bearing after his own time the sacred impress, not of Caesar,
But of God -

In the name of womanhood and humanity, I earnestly ask
That a general congress of women without limit of nationality,
May be appointed and held at someplace deemed most convenient
And the earliest period consistent with its objects,
To promote the alliance of the different nationalities,
The amicable settlement of international questions,
The great and general interests of peace.

Mothering Sunday was celebrated in Britain beginning in the 17th century, honored on the fourth Sunday in Lent. It began as a day when apprentices and servants could return home for the day to visit their mothers. They often brought a gift with them, often a "mothering cake" – a kind of fruitcake or fruit-filled pastry known as simnels. Furmety, a sweetened boiled cereal dish, was often served at the family dinner during Mothering Sunday celebrations. By the 19th century, the holiday had almost completely died out.

Mother's Day in Britain – or Mothering Sunday – came to be celebrated again after World War II, when American servicemen brought the custom and commercial enterprises used it as an occasion for sales, etc.

Mother's Day in America
Anna Jarvis, daughter of Anna Reeves Jarvis, stood at her mother's gravesite in 1905 and swore to dedicate her life to her mother's project, and establish a Mother's Day to honor mothers, living and dead. The activism she observed firsthand in her mother's fight to improve the living conditions of those battling poverty motivated her to carry on an activist project of her own: celebrating mothers who had come before her, mothers in her own lifetime, and mothers whose times had not yet come.

In 1907 Anna passed out 500 white carnations at her mother's church, St. Andrew's Methodist Episcopal Church in Grafton, West Virginia – one for each mother in the congregation.

On May 10, 1908, the first church–St. Andrew's in Grafton, West Virginia–responded to her request for a Sunday service honoring mothers. John Wanamaker, a Philadelphia merchant, joined the campaign for Mother's Day. That year, the first bill was presented in the U.S. Senate proposing establishment of Mother's Day, by Nebraska Senator Elmer Burkett, at the request of the Young Men's Christian Association. The proposal was killed by sending it back to committee, 33-14.

Yet, in 1909, Mother's Day services were held in 46 states plus Canada and Mexico.

Anna Jarvis gave up her job–to work full-time writing letters to politicians, clergy members, business leaders, women's clubs and anyone else she thought might have some influence. She was able to enlist the World's Sunday School Association in the lobbying campaign, a key success factor in convincing legislators in states and in the U.S. Congress to support the holiday.

In 1912, West Virginia became the first state to adopt an official Mother's Day, followed in 1914 with the U.S. Congress passing a Joint Resolution, President Woodrow Wilson signing it, establishing Mother's Day, emphasizing women's role in the family. Texas Senators Cotton Tom Heflin and Morris Shepard introduced the joint resolution adopted in 1914. Both were ardent prohibitionists.

Anna Jarvis became increasingly concerned over the overt commercialization of Mother's Day: "I wanted it to be a day of sentiment, not profit." She opposed the selling of flowers and also the use of greeting cards, saying these are "a poor excuse for the letter you are too lazy to write."

Anna Jarvis never had children of her own. She died in 1948, blind and penniless, and was buried next to her mother in a cemetery in the Philadelphia area.

Mother's Day Poem

A Mother is one who gives birth, but also nurtures.
A Mother is one who loves despite all your fault.
A Mother is one who kisses your boo-boos.
A Mother is one who also kicks your behind, when needed.
A Mother is one who gives you all the hugs and kisses in the world.
A Mother is one who knows you better than yourself.
A Mother is one who can relate to you in countless ways.
A Mother is one who also becomes a friend,
when the chid develops into an adult.
My Mother is all of these things and more.

Love, your daughter, Sara.

—Sara Nowlin—
Dedicated to mother Creda Nowlin

Mother's Day Statistics

• In the United States, there are about 82.5 million mothers.
(source: US Census Bureau)

• 96% of American consumers take part in some way in Mother's Day
(source: Hallmark)

• Mother's Day is widely reported as the peak day of the year for long
distance telephone calls

• Mother's Day is the busiest day of the year for many restaurants

• Retailers report that Mother's Day is the second highest gift-giving
holiday in the United States (Christmas is the highest)

• Most popular month for having babies in the US is August

• Most popular weekday for having babies in the US is Tuesday
(source: US Census Bureau)

• 82% of women in the US ages 40-44 are mothers in 2005
This compares to 90% in 1976 (source: US Census Bureau)

• In Utah and Alaska, women on the average will have three children
before the end of their childbearing years. Overall, the average in the
United States is two. (source: US Census Bureau)

• In 2002, the 55% of American women with infant children were in
the workforce, compared to 31% in 1976, and down from 59% in
1998. In 2002, there were 5.4 million stay-at-home mothers in the US.
(source: US Census Bureau)

Spend at least one Mother's Day with your respective mothers
before you decide on marriage. If a man gives his mother a gift
certificate for a flu shot, dump him.
—Erma Bombeck

Mother Nature

Human beings are not different from Nature, we are part of Nature.
Our very existence on earth depends on Nature. In truth, it is not we
who protect Nature, but Nature who protects us.
—Amma (Mother), Mata Amritanandamayi, India
Messages from Amma: In the Language of the Heart, www.amma.org

Nature is God made visible.
Nature is God known through our senses.
When we love and serve Nature, we are worshipping
the Supreme Being.
—Amma (Mother), Mata Amritanandamayi, India
Messages from Amma: In the Language of the Heart, www.amma.org

We are all connected to the one mother energy.
From time to time we need to remind ourselves of that to feel our
worth, how much we mean to those we know and to the universe.
—Linda Ferber

The power of nature to calm, heal and inspire is enormous for those
that take the time to look. The flaming clouds of a summer sunset;
the buttercup yellow of a full moon rising on a cloudless night;
mist sweeping up a valley; bird calls at dawn, all lift me beyond the
present, even if sometimes only for a moment.
—Anne Frodsham, Horticulturist, Nature lover, and Mother of two

Go outside. Leave the sidewalks behind.
—Cath Kachur, Speaker, Artist, ww.HumanTuneUp.com

Nature is beautiful. It is the basis of our survival. No nature, no us.
—Alison J. Roush, 8 years old and the saviour of all things living.

You can't get much closer to God than this!
—Wardene Weisser, Nature photographer, Mother of two
Grandmother of two

No One Could Have Told Me Then

When I became a mom, I was but a child you see
So low on self esteem at seventeen
Not able to imagine the joy that lie ahead
Unaware of the journey called life, some call it destiny
Would hold answers to a life long search
for love, for unconditional love
No one could have told me then.

So as I watched my little girl grow and saw
my own reflection through her eyes
striving to make her journey better, better than mine
Felt pretty complete when on the day, mission completed
My little girl grew into that woman and more
Than I ever imagined, what a joy!
Yet, no one could have told me then.

You see, I no longer searched for that elusive love
To fill me up inside and help me to shine
From the inside out, that's always been my truth
So, on this day I could not foresee
The miracle that lie ahead for me
When my daughter whispered those words in my ear
"Mom, I'm pregnant" she said.
Even then, no one could have told me.

Just after she arrived, I held her in my arms
Embraced her warmth in the nape of my neck
Moved through my body and soothed my soul
lifted me to a higher place, in just one embrace
I can still feel that first time we met
And still, no one could have told me then.

No one could have told me that my life would be changed
In such ways to end my life long search
For unconditional love
Through the birth of a child called Destiny
Who chose to call me "Ma"

No one could have told me then
Had to feel it for myself
Like when she would run and jump into my arms
Just because I came through the door
Allowed me to escape to a place in her embrace
Released the trigger holding all of my misguided fears
Of blowing the only chance at love I thought I had
Behind the many years of tears

No one could have told me then
That in a moment I would be set free
Free to create a new legacy
Through the eyes of this child called Destiny
My own destiny would unfold
Forever changed, forever love
No one could have told me then

—Patrice C. Baker, Speaker, Life Coach, Writer
www.ThePowerofWords.com

©2006 Patrice C. Baker

Or So I Thought

Dear mom,

You are GOD...or so I thought. For the first four years of my life you were an infallible being of perfection; an all knowing, all loving personification of divinity in a robe and slippers. By 1959 I was sure you always were and always would be, kind of like our nation felt about Dwight Eisenhower. You were the very genesis of my life. What else could you be if not GOD?

I remember much of the twenty years I spent under your roof. As a parent, you were a mix of timeless wisdom sprinkled with a little hypocrisy just to keep it real. Profanity would not be tolerated and you had a special affection for the third Commandment, "Thou shall keep holy the Lord's name." You admonished us should we use 'GOD' instead of 'Gosh' in our exclamations In the same evening one could hear you whisper a four-letter word as you absent-mindedly touched a hot pan on the stove without a potholder.

By 1964 I was already bigger than you were and I remember laughing when you attempted to dish out corporal punishment with a slap on my wrist. Your strongest blow had all the effect of a stiff breeze and I remember celebrating the moment. I was free of your influence. Or so I thought.

Actually, it is impossible to overstate your influence in my life. I have come to realize that every essential quality of my character came from you and the rest I learned in places and from people you warned me about. Your influence runs so deep I shutter to consider its depth. It is like molasses, sweet but irritatingly sticky.

Has a kid I resisted crossing my eyes out of fear of permanent damage. I still believe eating beets has a long-term health effect and to this day I carry all scissors and knives pointing down as if there is some real risk of falling while walking. Of course not all lessons are learned and if I ever stop cursing long enough someone should probably wash my mouth out with soap.

By the way, I know how close you came to cheating on dad. It was with Al Ferrara. It was now 1967 and I remember that summer afternoon when you almost crossed over the line, the third base line to be exact, to show your love for the left fielder of the Los Angeles

Dodgers. It was his bottom of the ninth, two-out home run that won the game that memorable day. With a swift swing of the bat he saved you the agony of having to explain to my friends and I that we would not be able to stay for extra innings as your dinner party beckoned. Leaving a ball game in progress would have been a fate worse than death to 12 year-olds and so as Ferrara rounded the bases to the sounds of a cheering crowd you mouthed "I love you" and we headed for the aisles. Don't worry, your secret is safe with me. I never told dad. I was happy you took us to the game but not nearly as appreciative as I should have been. After all, you loved baseball just has much as I did. Or so I thought.

I thought nothing could top landing on the moon and I watched it with you and dad on our black and white as Walter Cronkite gave us every detail, one step at a time. You were a proud American and taught me that patriotism really means being grateful for where you come from.

By 1975 I had learned many things. I discovered you did not love baseball as much as I did but loved me even more than I loved baseball. I came to realize your disappointment in me could hurt much more than any slap on the wrist. I learned GOD did not wear slippers and you were not perfect... or so I thought.

—R.D. Swineford
Dedicated to Elizabeth Swineford

Our Talks

Daughter	Hi Mama. How are you?
Mama	I love hearing from you - it's like you are here with me.
Daughter	The days are long without your voice to "cheer" me as it did as a little girl.

Laughter and tears
Lollipops and candy
A new doll and a teddy bear
The happy world of a little girl

Mama	I feel the same and I miss you too!
Daughter	You help me to find the answers to my problems as we talk each day.
Mama	I feel the same darling.
Daughter	The recipes and hints that you give me are wonderful.
Mama	It's wonderful that we have so much to share and that you make me part of your life.
Daughter	Even though we are miles apart our hearts are always together.
Mama	We have so much to remember such as the time when you wanted to jump down the stairs and were afraid you would fall and I said "Don't give up". Then you jumped and you were pleased and so was I. There have been so many times that we cheered each other on. I love your life in the arts and it has been a "big' part of our lives. It has been hard being an artist but I still say to this day "Don't give up."
Daughter	I also remember the family joke about your purse and I wrote a poem when I was a teen and it said:

Mommy's Purse
Tissues, lipstick, mints,
Bandaids, gums, candy bars
Everything you need plus
Love, Kisses and Hugs

Mama	Yes Sweetheart that is true. I always carry a lot in my purse. Also memories of Halloween reminded me of you as a child.

HALLOWEEN

The house is dark and quiet.
Outside the light shines bright.
The carved pumpkin smiles
in the dark and mysterious night.

The chocolates and candles are on the tray
awaiting the arrival of goblins and ghosts
who will eagerly sing out "Trick or treat"
to their awaiting hosts.

The doorbell begins to ring.
Flashlights glow in the dark.
The little devil grins in his red suit,
clutching his long tail;
The princess in white satin
waving her wand;
The boy as a dog dressed in blue.

All sing out "Thank you" for the treats.
Mothers and fathers carry the little ones
Themselves dressed in holiday hue
smile as the tots laugh and coo.

HAPPY HALLOWEEN TO ALL
AND TO ALL A GOOD NIGHT.

Daughter	I also remember your singing to me at night and to me you had the most beautiful voice in the world.
Mama	Thank you darling.
Daughter	Anytime I've had a bad day you encourage me not to get discouraged. You have helped me be the person I am today.
Mama	Dad and I are very proud of you.
Daughter	Goodnight Mama Kisses and I love you.
Mama	Goodnight Daughter Kisses and I love you too and enjoy our wonderful talks

—Lillian Berman (mother) and Selena Parker-Berman (daughter)

Parenting

For mothers, it can be an endless routine task.
Parenting can be quite a trying job, especially if you have a handful of boisterous bundles of destructive energy. It takes more than your mettle to deal with the minute-to-minute parenting.

Any mother could perform the jobs of several air traffic controllers with ease.
—Lisa Alther

She never quite leaves her children at home,
even when she doesn't take them along.
—Margaret Culkin Banning

You see much more of your children once they leave home.
—Lucille Ball, Comedienne

No one ever died from sleeping in an unmade bed.
I have known mothers who remake the bed after their children do it because there's a wrinkle in the spread or the blanket is on crooked. This is sick.
—Erma Bombeck

You can fool all of the people some of the time,
and some of the people all of the time, but You Can't Fool Mom.
—Captain Penny's Law

Don't expect your children to do anything you won't do for yourself.
—Colette Carlson, Speaker, Author, mother of two teenage daughters

There are two lasting bequests we can give our children.
One is roots. The other is wings.
—Hodding Carter, Jr.

In spite of the six thousand manuals on child raising in the
bookstores, child raising is still a dark continent and no one really
knows anything. You just need a lot of love and luck - and, of course,
courage.
—Bill Cosby, *Fatherhood*

No matter how calmly you try to referee, parenting will eventually
produce bizarre behavior, and I'm not talking about the kids.
—Bill Cosby, *Fatherhood*

If you have never been hated by your child,
you have never been a parent.
—Bette Davis

It would seem that something which means poverty, disorder
and violence every single day should be avoided entirely,
but the desire to beget children is a natural urge.
—Phyllis Diller

There actually was a time I was a perfect parent and I knew all the
answers —then, the first baby came along and suddenly I realized I
didn't even know what the questions were.
—Rita Emmett - Recovering Procrastinator
Author *The Procrastinating Child: A Handbook for Adults to Help
Children Stop Putting Things Off* www.RitaEmmett.com

Don't worry that children never listen to you;
worry that they are always watching you.
—Robert Fulghum

Parents often talk about the younger generation
as if they didn't have anything to do with it.
—Haim Ginott

The beauty of "spacing" children many years apart lies in the fact that
parents have time to learn the mistakes that were made with the
older ones - which permits them to make exactly the opposite
mistakes with the younger ones.
—Sydney J. Harris

Your children need your presence more than your presents.
—Reverend Jesse Jackson

If there is anything that we wish to change in the child,
we should first examine it and see whether it is not something
that could better be changed in ourselves.
—Carl Jung, *Integration of the Personality*, 1939

People either imitate or make vows not to be like their parents.
—Cath Kachur, Speaker, Artist, www.HumanTuneUp.com

Whenever I held my newborn baby in my arms, I used to think that
what I said and did to him could have an influence not only on him
but on all whom he met, not only for a day or a month or a year, but
for all eternity - a very challenging and exciting thought for a mother.
—Rose Kennedy

You will always be your child's favorite toy.
—Vicki Lansky, *Trouble-Free Travel with Children*, 1991

Insanity is hereditary - you get it from your kids.
—Sam Levenson

By and large, mothers and housewives are the only workers who do
not have regular time off. They are the great vacationless class.
—Anne Morrow Lindbergh

If I Had My Child To Raise Over Again
If I had my child to raise all over again,
I'd build self-esteem first, and the house later.
I'd finger-paint more, and point the finger less.
I would do less correcting and more connecting.
I'd take my eyes off my watch, and watch with my eyes.
I'd take more hikes and fly more kites.
I'd stop playing serious, and seriously play.
I would run through more fields and gaze at more stars.
I'd do more hugging and less tugging.
—Diane Loomans, Speaker, Author, Mother
From *If I Had My Child To Raise Over Again*

It's not only children who grow. Parents do too. As much as we watch to see what our children do with their lives, they are watching us to see what we do with ours. I can't tell my children to reach for the sun. All I can do is reach for it, myself.
—Joyce Maynard

Ma-ma does everything for the baby,
who responds by saying Da-da first.
—Mignon McLaughlin, *The Second Neurotic's Notebook*

It's never too late to be a better parent. Start today.
Model the behavior you wish to see in your children.
Discipline with wisdom and gentleness.
Love freely and openly, expressing often and in many ways
how you cherish and value each of your children,
just as God treasures each of us.
—Mary Manin Morrissey, Author *Life Keys*

Sing out loud in the car even, or especially,
if it embarrasses your children.
—Marilyn Penland

Like all parents, my husband and I just do the best we can,
hold our breath and hope we've set aside enough money
for our kid's therapy.
—Michelle Pfeiffer, Actress, Mother

You have a lifetime to work, but children are only young once.
—Polish Proverb

Teach your children to choose the right path,
and when they are older, they will remain upon it.
—Proverbs 22:6

Children are our second chance to have a great parent-child relationship.
—Dr. Laura Schlessinger

If there is love, there is no such thing as being too tough with a child.
—Sandra Schrift, proud Grandmother

Having kids—the responsibility of rearing good, kind, ethical,
responsible human beings—the biggest job anyone can embark on.
Like any risk, you have to take a leap of faith and ask lots of
wonderful people for their help and guidance. I thank God everyday
for giving me the opportunity to parent.
—Maria Kennedy Shriver Schwarzenegger,
as interviewed in *O Magazine* by Oprah Winfrey

Though motherhood is the most important of all the professions –
requiring more knowledge than any other department in human
affairs – there was no attention given to preparation for this office.
—-Elizabeth Cady Stanton

Making the decision to have a child is momentous.
It is to decide forever to have your heart go walking
around outside your body.
—Elizabeth Stone

I guess I am a little sensitive to the Army slogan
"The toughest job, you will ever love!"
They obviously know nothing about being a parent.
—Judy Tejwani

Parents must get across the idea that "I love you always,
but sometimes I do not love your behavior."
—Amy Vanderbilt, Author, authority on manners and etiquette

And so our mothers and grandmothers have, more often than not
anonymously, handed on the creative spark, the seed of the flower
they themselves never hoped to see – or like a sealed letter they could
not plainly read.
—Alice Walker

When you put faith, hope and love together,
you can raise positive kids in a negative world.
—Zig Ziglar, Motivational Speaker, Author

Make Every Stranger Your Friend

In a world that now teaches fear and distrust, my mother lived a life that turned every stranger into a friend. Growing up as a child in the 50's, I longed for a mother more like June Cleaver in the TV show, *Leave it to Beaver.* Instead, I got *Auntie Mame.*

Unlike the stay-at-home moms, my mother, Mickey, was flamboyant and outgoing. She would talk to everyone, anywhere and about anything. And, amazingly, people responded. Her friends were affluent yet my mother preferred to wear costume jewelry and hand-me-down clothing. She shared her wealth with others, never missing an opportunity to give a gift or celebrate someone else's success. She loved to entertain and was extraordinary at it. It did not matter how great the food or what time it was served; her guests left happy and engaged. Despite numerous family tragedies, my mother maintained life-long friendships and made new friends along the way. She had a network that extended to every walk of life; always introducing people with positive results. As a speaker and author on the topic of networking, I have hopefully found a way to share her legacy by helping others recognize the power of a single connection. My mother believed that there are no strangers, only friends you have not met. Now her legacy lives on through her family, their work and the lives they touch.

—Cindy Chernow

A MOTHER'S WISH

I want to share with him
The truths of the world as I know them
And those I have yet to learn
To protect him from the pain
That he may endure on his journey
To carry the light that leads his way
While his small hands clutch to mine
To watch his smile
To hear his laugh
To share all my love
To never miss a moment of this
Is a Mother's only wish

—Tina Rubin—

PTA MOM

My role as a mother is absolutely wonderful. I would have never imagined–when I experience the first little flutter inside me–the challenges, the special moments, discovering your child's individual personality, being patient, the many roles that you must play, and most important, the LOVE that you have in your heart for your children. Sometimes, it does not seem real and as time goes by, it seems that I have fewer moments to make the best impressions for them. I strive to ensure that they have faith, healthy values, respect for themselves and others, be accountable for their actions/decisions, cherish their life, protect their siblings and stay grounded. You learn the acts of motherhood through "trial and error" and pray that your children will make the right choices in life.

One role that I am pleased with is my role and involvement in the school PTA. It has been so fun and amazing. Although very time-consuming, I have had the opportunity to spend time with my children at school; work extremely close with their teachers; know their friends; and continue to be the parent advocate that I must be. As a parent, I owe it to my children to provide them with the best education and becoming a part of their school PTA has helped with providing them the support and growth they need. I also get a kick out of my 7-year old son sharing with his friends that he has perks, because his mommy is the PTA President.

I see my children - not only - as a reflection of my future but also a reflection of my past. I am so truly thankful that God has blessed me to become a mother, and equally blessed to have my children in my life!

—Tina Holmes

Once A Mother, Always A Mother

For I realized that the process of mothering, as described in a man's world, supposed children at an age to be 'mothered' in the home. But the reality of mothering goes on throughout the entire life of the mother. A bad mother might make a good grandmother. Once a mother, always a mother - even if your daughter is seventy. The relationship changes, of course, but is no less important.

—Rachel Billington, From the *Sunday Times*, March 13, 1994

Looking Back At My Mothers And All Mothers

While I am certain now that I was always loved by both my mother and my great aunt, who did much of the day-to-day rearing, it was my aunt who gave the "warm fuzzies" that most associate with mom. It wasn't always so and this confused me in my early years.

Mother went off to work, had a second career as a model and a life. My aunt stayed home and cared for her brothers and me. And I wondered when I saw traditional, nuclear, families what was really normal. Television was the new sensation. I remember both Harriet Nelson and Donna Reed and it is in their image that I, and many others of my generation with working mothers, forged our early views of just what a mother should be - and somehow knowing that we didn't have one. Those friends who had a stay-at-home mom were envied.

This is not to criticize my aunt. She was terrific. A "better" mother didn't exist on the planet. But there was a gap in the blood-line, a disconnect that couldn't be ignored, or supplanted fully. Like Catholic School, I survived it and may have been stronger for it. I know that's true of many others, as well. Life goes on. We grow up. We start our own families and the cycle goes on but it is always informed by what happened with mother way back when.

There are times, when I see them as clearly as if they were standing in front of me. I feel them when certain triggers are pulled. My aunt, I called her Pooh, comes to mind whenever I smell a particularly savory apple pie or roast of beef. When I see a woman strike a particularly elegant pose, my mother, her nickname is Igor, and her days in modeling flash before me. I don't try to have these thoughts, they are woven into my fabric and they bubble up.

Which brings me to scars. Mothers get them from their children - my mother, for example, still blames me for ruining her bladder for her later years by kicking up a storm in the womb - some are based on real disappointments, real pain. Other scars come from expectations gone awry. And children get their scars, as well.

I have long-since forgiven my mother and my aunt for their shortfalls as parents. In turn, they have forgiven me for never being the son they first contemplated and envisioned (they wanted a lawyer). We have all learned from history, that there are few hero's journeys that end up where you first expect them to go, and fewer superhero (or heroine) costumes that fit as well at 50 as they do at 17. I suspect we have all received value in the end.

In talking about motherhood, I often say, "motherhood is a terminalillness." It changes a woman. I have never found a woman for whom that isn't true and in marrying women with children I always knew, deep down, where their loyalties lay and tried not ever to put the mother in a position of choosing.

When I think of mothers, I think of hearts put into an endless journey, proud hearts beating with great expectations for their children to be better, stronger, more... than they. I can feel their frustrations when the child doesn't meet expect-ation, or when the child merely stumbles and fear for safety is replaced by "be more careful!" Of their hearts breaking when the child faces crisis, or simply when s/he can't be protected anymore. And, of hearts swelling with pride when the child does something splendid, or ordinary, and all that work flashes through.

Yet this I know, I wouldn't be the person, the friend, the lover, the partner, the citizen, or the man that I am today had they not been there at the beginning and throughout my life. Even today, as I approach 60, I feel their words, actions and hearts intruding (Mothers intrude, others interrupt. There's nothing for it and you just have to get used to it.) at the strangest moments - still guiding, or trying to, after all these years. What a gift.

—John Reddish

May I Have This Dance?

How do people from dysfunctional homes know what is normal or appropriate in relationships? What happens if you want to be a loving parent but your role model was a bad example? How do you learn to be a mother if you have never been mothered?

As a parent educator, I have been blessed to work with groups of people from all over the world who want to enhance their parenting skills or find help in the midst of crisis. None reinforced the choice of my calling as did a participant a few years ago.

Regardless of the subject, a beautiful young woman continued to show up at my weekly parenting class. She slipped into a seat in the back of the room and took volumes of notes but refused to participate in group discussions.

Attendees varied from being court assigned, some child care providers looking for additional training, and parents who wanted to learn about a specific topic. She never signed the roster or filled out an evaluation. She always rushed out of class while I was visiting with others, so I never got an opportunity to get to know her on a one-to-one basis.

Then one night, I shared the story of a foster daughter coming into the kitchen when my husband and I were dancing to a tune on the radio. Becky collapsed on the chair and sobbed, "I never knew parents danced together. I knew they fought and argued and threw things, but I didn't know they laughed and enjoyed each other and their children."

We were stunned and heartbroken. It never occurred to us that living in a normal household was almost like living in a foreign country to her. We consoled her, "Oh Sweetheart. We are so sorry you had to see people be unkind to you and one another. You didn't deserve that and it wasn't your fault."

"Someday," she vowed, "I want to have a man who will dance me around the kitchen." We promised her that she would, and she did.

After others left the class that night, my mystery participant approached me and requested a few minutes of my time. When we sat down, she asked if I would hug her. I told her what an honor and privilege it would be and how much I admired her diligence in attending the parenting classes.

She then told me she came, not because she had children or worked with children, but because she had never been allowed to be a child. Her mother was mentally ill and from the time she was 7 years old, she was the adult in the family. She had been forced to assume the role of caretaker for herself, younger siblings, her ill mother and drunken father when he showed up.

She confessed her need to mentally establish what normal families were like, before she could trust herself to get serious in a relationship. Her early life had been so chaotic and like Becky in the story, she was not sure what mothers or children did in a family setting. She decided if all families were as dysfunctional as her family of origin, she would never marry.

Connecting with this story, she decided she too wanted a man who would dance with her in the kitchen, honor her forever and help in the parenting process. She decided she would go out with the kind, wonderful colleague who had been pursuing her for months.

The classes helped her recognize the chaos had not been her fault and she had done the best she could under the circumstances. Each week, she would review notes from the class and ask herself, "Can you do this?" Her confidence and knowledge grew as more and more often, the answer was yes!

She is now a wife and mother and doing such a good job. I'm always pleased when she shows up for parenting classes. Now she has lots of techniques, tips and contributions to share on having a happy cooperative family.

The highlight of seeing her again is when she hugs me and says "I danced in the kitchen today."

—Judy H. Wright, Speaker, Author, Parent Educator
© Judy H. Wright
www.artichokepress.com

Perfect Parents

The Missing Car

One day I was driving into a parking lot of a shopping center and my mother was standing there looking confused and upset. I drove up to her and asked what was wrong. She said she had driven her Cadillac there and upon leaving the store she could not find her car in the lot. I told her to get in my car and I would drive her around the parking lot to look for it. "Mom, you must have just forgotten where you parked." She became more incensened by the moment.

As we drove around, we came upon my parents other vehicle, a Ford Taurus. It was obviously their's because they bought it from a relative and his name was on the license plate holder. "You just forgot which car you brought and where you parked it, it's no big deal," I offered. In trying to make her feel better, she only became more annoyed as I spoke. She blurts out, "I'm sure I didn't bring this car and I know I was parked over there!" Still trying to humor her, the glares are getting icier. At that moment, my father came screeching up behind us in their Cadillac and he was laughing.

He explained that he had driven to a store in the same shopping center. After making his purchase and exiting the store, he saw the Cadillac first. Forgetting that he brought the Ford, he jumped in to drive home. When he was half way home, he realized that the things on the passenger seat of the car were not there on his way to the store. Then it hit him, he had the wrong car! When he drove up, my mom was so angry at him for taking the car and me for not believing her story, that she just got in it and drove home.

We have never heard the end of this story. I think she is still mad.

Not really, she's my mom–and she's perfect!!!

—Linda Lev
In tribute to my mother Garnet Brassfield

✳ 193 ✳

Prayer

MY DAILY PRAYER

If I can do some good today,
If I can serve along life's way,
If I have something helpful say,
Lord, show me how.
If I can right a human wrong,
If I can help to make one strong,
If I can cheer with smile or song,
Lord, show me how.
If I can aid one in distress,
If I can make a burden less,
If I can spread more happiness,
Lord, show me how.

— Unknown —

A Goddess Prayer

Thank you for the eternal beauty that I know I am.
For giving me the energy to create life and know I can create
anything else.
I accept graciously the abundance I am blessed with and look joyfully
forward to sharing it with others.
Love surrounds me. My life is filled with magic. My spirit dances
freely.
I am forever grateful and in awe of the wonders of the world.
As I take a few moments to sit in peace, I embrace the silence and
listen with deep respect because I know you hear me and it is then I'll
find the answers to my prayers.
Thanks you for listening, loving and being forever there.

—Wanda Lee Miller—

OUR PRAYER FOR OUR CHILDREN

Children of the Light - as you walk into your school, down the hall, into your classroom, to the playground, into your library, and lunch places - we promise to hold you in Love's embrace and massively comfort you with our watchful thoughts and prayers. We promise to remember that you come from Love. You go in Love, speak in Love, and move in Love. You ARE Love. Thank you for who you are.

The appearance of your smallness does not fool us into thinking that you are vulnerable. We see your spiritual strength and power as your divine inheritance. We see you in Love's embrace, forever safe. We know that the angels of care are causing you to think according to your true identity, to be in your appointed place of dignity, worth, preciousness, and power — protected while you go about your business of good. We are with you.

You, our cherished children, are in the healing light of Love. We want you to know that we are assuring you by our continual watchful and loving thoughts for you. Our prayers will be the footprints of Love all around you, throughout the day. You will feel them. You will know them. They will be present with you, keeping you safe and secure. We will keep our sacred watch for you. You — all of you — are our children. Not one of you is outside our love.

Please know how much we care. We promise to pause for moments throughout our day to remember who you are – to honor your divinity. Please feel our hugs surrounding you, our kisses celebrating you. Please hear our messages of love for you.

Let us whisper to you this prayer of Love. Feel it to your toes. Let your heart sing with happiness, play, and safety. Hear our prayer. You are irreplaceable. You are magnificent. You are our wonders. Go in Love's way. Love is holding you in Her care, every waking moment, even as you rest your sweet head, on Love's pillow of peace. We love you and always will.

—Shannon Peck is co-founder of TheLoveCenter, a non-profit educational organization dedicated to bringing all humanity into the heart of Love. She is a co-author of *The Love You Deserve, Liberating Your Magnificence,* with husband Dr. Scott Peck.

Precious Child

Seen Through the Eyes of Love and Light

As women it is essential to our well-being and absolute joy to be in connection with our inner child. It is our inner child that finds the joy and laughter in the every day things. It is our childlike nature that allows us to be silly and full of life. She is able to be as loud as she wants and many times will sing at the top of her lungs. She is the part of us that lets us dance around the house in our underwear. She is always open for new adventure and feels no fear or limitations.

Many women have forgotten that beautiful child that still lives within. The little child loses her zest for life a little bit at a time when she is told to be a certain way. When the small child is not seen for who she is she tries to please and becomes something different. When the child is not allowed to be exactly who she, she loses her light.

When we are seen for we are and allowed to be exactly who we are, we feel empowered.

It is difficult to cultivate a feeling within yourself when you don't know what it feels like. It is difficult to feel thin if you have always felt fat. There is one woman in in my life who encouraged and allowed me to be a child. Because I knew what it felt like, I am now able to connect back to my inner child. It is when I am connected to my inner child that I am connected to pure joy. It is when I am connected with my adult self, my inner child and God that I am fulfilled.

It has been said that the way you hold a person in your mind is the way that they will ultimately behave. School teachers that have admiration and confidence in a child will witness that child bloom and grow and live up to their expectations. This child will excel because the teacher believes in her. If you take the same child and put her in a classroom where the teacher is critical and has a low opinion of that child, she will perform at that level as well. This child will not live up to her true potential and many times fail. The way we are held in the minds of our parents, grandparents, teachers, and even Godparents will shape and mold our self-esteem and self-confidence.

I am blessed that many years ago my wonderful mother chose Marianne to be my Godmother. Marianne has the most amazing, beautiful and loving heart. She is evidence to me that angels are walking among us. She is kind, nurturing, and accepting. She never speaks a harsh word about anyone. And she lacks judgment. No matter how I felt about myself, my godmother always reflected to me that I was precious, loving, and a beautiful angel. I felt so loving in her presence. I felt love and appreciation for myself. I felt connected to my inner being. I felt love.

Many of us understand what unconditional love means, and have witnessed this type of love in our lives. However, I have never encountered a Spirit other than Marianne that truly gives consistent unconditional love. She has four children and a number of grand-children and I'm sure they would all agree that in her eyes you are perfect just as you are. There is such a sense of allowing that emanates from her. She sees the perfection of God within each of us and reminds us of that perfection in her beautiful, loving, and com-passionate blue eyes. You cannot help but to flourish in her presence.

A child needs to be accepted and shown true connection. They need to feel safe. They need to be told that they are precious angels. They need to be reminded of the love that they are by looking into the eyes of those that love them. They need to know that they can dream and be encouraged to go after those dreams.

I was not considered a "perfect" child by those in my family. I often did not meet their pictures of what a child was supposed to do. I did not eat. I did not sleep. I often cried. I often did the opposite of what I was told to do. I was called "A pain in the ass."

One day when I was only a year-and-a-half, Marianne was changing my diaper. I believe that because I was told that I was "a pain in the ass" by those that loved me, that meant "I love you." While Marianne was changing my diaper, I looked up at her with love in my eyes and said, "Marianne, you're a pain in the ass."

This tribute is to a woman that always allows me to be myself. She never criticizes or judges me. She only sees my positive aspects and that is all I ever show her, because in her presence I am pure love. I can see that precious child within because she showed me what she looked like. This is the greatest gift I was given from my Godmother and because of her I am who I am today.

—Christy Whitman, best-selling author of *Perfect Pictures: An Inspirational Book for Those Who Like it Perfect and Why Did She Choose Suicide*
www.christywhitman.com

Pregnancy

QUESTION & ANSWER

Q: I'm two months pregnant now.
   When will my baby move?
A: With any luck, right after he finishes college.

Q: My wife is five months pregnant and so moody that
   sometimes she's borderline irrational.
A: So, what's your question?

Q: My childbirth instructor says it's not pain I'll feel during labor,
   but pressure. Is she right?
A: Yes, in the same way that a tornado might be called an air current.

Q: When is the best time to get an epidural?
A: Right after you find out you're pregnant.

Q: Our baby was born last week.
   When will my wife begin to feel and act normal again?
A: When the kids are in college.

Think of stretch marks as pregnancy service stripes.
—Joyce Armor

You should never say anything to a woman that even remotely
suggests that you think she's pregnant unless you can see an actual
baby emerging from her at that moment.
—Dave Barry, *Things That It Took Me 50 Years to Learn*

There are three reasons for breast-feeding:
the milk is always at the right temperature;
it comes in attractive containers; and the cat can't get it.
—Irena Chalmers

By far the most common craving of pregnant women
is not to be pregnant.
—Phyllis Diller, Comedienne

If pregnancy were a book they would cut the last two chapters.
—Nora Ephron, *Heartburn*, 1983

It is now possible for a flight attendant to get a pilot pregnant.
—Richard J. Ferris, President of United Airlines

The spiritual quality of earth: eternally pregnant and containing
in its fertility the unwritten cipher of cosmic lore.
—Lady Frieda Harris, English artist

If nature had arranged that husbands and wives should have children
alternatively, there would never be more than three in a family.
—Lawrence Housman

In the sheltered simplicity of the first days after a baby is born,
one sees again the magical closed circle, the miraculous sense
of two people existing only for each other.
—Anne Morrow Lindbergh

I didn't know how babies were made
until I was pregnant with my fourth child.
—Loretta Lynn

Life is tough enough without having someone kick you
from the inside.
—Rita Rudner

Curve:
The loveliest distance between two points.
—Mae West

Raising Spiritually - Centered Kids

Being a mother is much more than making sure your kid's physical and emotional needs are met. It seems to me that a child is much more balanced when their spiritual needs have been considered and given a high priority. To me spiritual doesn't have to be any specific religion. It is a knowingness deep within you. As an adult I am constantly learning about Spirit and what it means to me.

So many times we neglect to give our children the opportunity to learn how to live in "Spirit." We think they are too young, or we don't know how to get "it" across to them, or that "they" just won't understand, that it is too complex or that they will think we are "weird."

It's not our job to make that judgment call for them. We need to go out on that limb and introduce spirituality to them by describing what it means to us. They will absorb what their spirit wants them to know at the time. They will in turn decide what their spirituality means to them.

I took my children to a spiritual retreat a couple of years ago with amazing results. They do get "it"... they really do. As a result, they do meditations with me... they talk with me... and we pull Angel cards on a daily basis (they look forward to it). We talk about our problems. They feel that home is a safe place to take risks.

My daughter really started opening up after that retreat. She used to be afraid of many things. At that retreat, in that quiet place in her soul, she learned that she didn't have to be afraid. Her Spirit told her.

At the retreat we learned to live in the light. We learned that good things happen when we look at thing positively and when we look at things negatively it seems that things go wrong.

A couple of months after the retreat my son, my daughter and I were sitting around a lit candle, each holding in our hands a heart made out of a gemstone. We usually ask if anyone has something they want to share and my son did.

He held his heart to the light and said. "When we bring our heart to the light the world is brighter." Then he pulled the heart away from the candle and said "When we move our heart away from the light our world gets darker." He knew to live with "Spirit - The Light."

We can never judge when someone is "old" enough or "ready" enough to be introduced to spirituality. It is our job as mothers, as parents, as spiritual beings to introduce the information. The child will decide if he or she is ready. I know this because my daughter was 9 and my son was 6 and they were both ready (and undoubtedly ready at birth).

—Debbi McGill, Mother of two, business owner

CARDS OF LOVE – CHILDREN THANK THEIR MOTHER

Justin, Age 14
Mom for the past fourteen years of my life we have had so many memories. My gratitude for your love and wisdom is everlasting. Though you have taught me many things I know I still have a lot to learn. But I have learned how to work hard and be loving and never give up. You have shown me the light and I am very grateful. You don't have to worry I will teach these lessons to my kids and I will hopefully also show them the light. So happy birthday mom from your son to you, and no matter what, you know that I love you, Justin

Cassie age 12
I love the way you smile and the way you take the time to listen, even if it's one of my stories. I wish I could give you the world, but I can't, so here's a simple kiss and thank you for all you have done for me. And remember that my kiss never will fade of wash from your hand!

You're my hero because you think of everyone before yourself everyday. I remember when we lived in LA and you would drive from work in San Diego to LA just to be there for us when we needed you and then go back to work that same day. You're my hero because you teach us to love ourselves and others for whom we are. I hope I can be a hero just like you when I grow up.
Love, Cassie

P.S. Thank you for being my hero.
—Proud Mother Ave Maria Rubenstein

Rent an Aunt

I was not blessed to be a mother; God had better ideas for me.
I was a "Rent an Aunt!!"

It all started with the twins, Brian and Michael. I would take them to
the local church carnival, the mall, or hang out at home watching a
movie. This gave their parents Rod and Diane an hour or two free
which parents of twins sorely need from time to time.

I then progressed to being a natural Aunt to my brother Bob's
daughter Annie. Every Friday night she would pull her little chair up in
front of their big picture window and watch for me. She was my "hot"
Friday night date. Her folks would go out to dinner and a movie while
we had wonderful adventures. Later in years she would travel with
me to Ireland, Alaska, Las Vegas, and Mexico. I like to think I inspired
her love of travel!

Then there were the Johnson kids. Scott, Kathleen and Tim were
raised in a close-knit family of meager means. They knew not what
room service was all about until "Aunt" Becky showed them the
wonders of a Sheraton Hotel!!! With me they learned there is more to
life but one must earn it.

Today all my "kids" are productive, happy, lovely human beings.
I have danced at their weddings, held their babies and have kept
in touch with them although miles may separate us.

I like to think that maybe, just maybe by being a "Rent an Aunt"
I made an impact on them in some small way!!

—Becky Palmer

Second Chances

We all deserve second chances. That's what I have always been told, actually, my Dad's way of putting it is: "We all make mistakes, that's why they put erasers on pencils." And that's what I wanted to believe. But when you have done something unforgivable, when society lets you know they don't approve of your choice, it can be difficult to allow yourself that second chance.

I was married at 19 to an older man, and became a mother at 22. I adored my son, a fellow Aquarian; we seemed to have the same nature. When he was 5, I left. I left my husband, but in the end, I left my son, too. Without going into the details, I hadn't intended to leave my son with his father, it evolved into that choice. For reasons I prefer not to go into, largely because they are irrelevant to this story, it felt to me at 27, that I either left, or I would die. It sounds simplistic, but it was so intense a feeling that even now, 18 years later, I can still remember the waves of depression, fear, and self-loathing. I couldn't stay, but I had thought my son would come with me. And then, he didn't. My ex-husband wanted custody, so I fought for joint custody, with our son living with his father.

So began a 4 year period of separation, partly due to an acrimonious divorce, and partly due to my work, which kept me out of state. There were visits, summers, holidays, but not enough. I was not there.

When I could finally return home, I was able to be more a part of my son's life, but still, work kept me in another town. And then one day, after meeting the man who would become my second husband, I KNEW that no matter what, I had to go back, face my ex and try to live in the same town. My son was now 14, if I didn't go back, I would lose him forever.

Would I get a second chance to be a full-time mom? I would be there, but would my son want me there? The answer is not easy, as now he had to choose all the time between me and my ex-husband. It was not pretty, but I was determined. The transition was difficult, my new husband was amazing, supportive, a calming influence on all of us. But the greatest hurdle I had was the guilt. All those years of being the visiting parent. No matter how much women have achieved, mothers who leave are not popular. Those who knew my son and his father had their opinions, some were vocal about it, others just silently condemning.

Second chances, to show up and earn the respect and trust of my child. Would I leave again? Could he really count on me? I knew I had done a pretty good job of part time parenting, not as good as some, but I stayed involved in his life. There were fights, tearful apologies, healing conversations. And slowly, I began to realize that the forgiveness I was seeking was my own. I had to forgive myself, first, before any true connection to my son could be made. When I did let the past go, it was as if a huge weight fell off both of our shoulders.

The teenage years had their challenges, as they all do. But we got through them. Even my ex and I realized a united front was the best course on school and other issues. We made it work.

My son will graduate college this year after a full-ride Division 1 basketball scholarship. He is an amazing human being, a talented athlete and a loving son. I have been given my second chance, in spades. I will not squander it.

Oh, and because the Universe is kind, I was blessed with another second chance, as my husband and I welcomed our own son, now 3, when I was 42 years old.

I have learned, keep learning, keep reaching for more connection and more compassion for myself, for those who I meet who have had to make hard choices. I give my son the benefit of my 20/20 hindsight, knowing it is his path, his choice that really counts.

Second chances do happen, if you show up for them.

—Anonymous, by request

Securi-Tea

Tea Prayer

The surety of God provides me
with the security of God.
God is all there is, and
God is all the protection I need.
With this Presence, I am safe;
with this Power, I am whole,
and we are one.

I am certain in God; this is God's guarantee.
This makes us one for all eternity.
A divine promise whispered to me
one day while sipping hot tea.
I am now free from all agony and fear.
I am secure in my being
and confident in my good.

My future is assured, insured and secured.
I am grateful for the gift of this word.
I am safe and guarded by this holy shield.
I know no danger and no stranger.
We are all one when we surrender
to the Real One.
And so it is.

Amen

—Darlene Fahl-Brittian—
Certified Tea Specialist
Sipping Tea - Celebrating Me
www.TakeUpTheCup.com

Sereni-Tea

Tea Prayer

In peaceful repose,
I breathe in all that I am.
I marvel in the simplicity
and purity of divine serenity.
From this place of perfection I am undisturbed.
I am calm and refreshed, most unperturbed.

I see God, I feel God, I hear the word.
Clearly and calmly,
I am one with this Force.
I am intact; I am whole, pure and good.
I see the reflection of my own perfection,
no defects and no deficiencies.

Nothing can diminish the goodness and the Godness of me.
In serenity and with deep gratitude
I realize God is all of me from within me.
So with ease and grace I surrender my pace.
I have nothing to fear; there is no race.

No rush, no hurry, no finish line.
Every day I know victory in the arms of the Divine -
my giver, my deliverer, the provider of bliss.

I need for nothing; the aches are all gone.
My soul is free to be all that it is -
love is all it can be,
and that's good enough for me.

Amen

—Darlene Fahl-Brittian—
Certified Tea Specialist
Sipping Tea - Celebrating Me
www.TakeUpTheCup.com

Sense of Self

When you know you are the Self, you are like a giant battery
connected to a cosmic power supply providing constant,
inexhaustible strength... your energy never diminishes;
you draw from an infinite potential... Think of God as your own Self.
—Amma (Mother), Mata Amritanandamayi, India
Messages from Amma: In the Language of the Heart, www.amma.org

Love yourself first and everything else falls into line.
You have to really love yourself to get anything done in this world.
—Lucille Ball, Comedienne

You grow up the day you have your first real laugh, at yourself.
—Ethel Barrymore

Let the world know you as you are, not as you think you should be...
—Fanny Brice

Your work is to discover your world and then with all your heart
give yourself to it.
—Buddha

You yourself, as much as anybody in the entire universe,
deserve your love and affection.
—Buddha

When your heart speaks, take good notes.
—Judith Campbell

If there is light in the soul, there will be beauty in the person.
If there is beauty in the person, there will be harmony in the house.
If there is harmony is the house, there will be order in the nation.
If there is order in the nation, there will be peace in the world.
—Chinese Proverb

The minute you settle for less than you deserve,
you get even less than you settled for.
—Maureen Dowd

Life's lessons never end. A lesson is repeated until learned.
—Cath Kachur, Speaker, Artist, www.HumanTuneUp.com

Men look *at* themselves in mirrors.
Women look *for* themselves.
—Elissa Melamed

Self-esteem is only one of the factors that should be considered
when we look to develop ourselves. Another factor is self-acceptance
including loving ourselves, or at least not negatively judging ourselves, when we feel helpless, inferior and vulnerable. Self-esteem
alone does not determine your ability to live your life fully. You are
a unique human being. You should know what is good about you,
accept your strengths and carry them with you into the world.
Love who you are becoming.
—Marcia Reynolds, MCC, Speaker, Author *Capture the Rapture:
How to Step Out of Your Head and Leap Into Life*

No one can make you feel inferior without your consent.
—Eleanor Roosevelt

Work on bringing out a special trait that you admire about yourself
and don't let anyone stop you from being like that.
—Michelle C. Roush, age 16, From an essay entitled *To Be Free*

Think highly of yourself, for the world takes you
at your own estimate.
—Unknown

The whole point of being alive is to evolve into the complete person
you were intended to be.
—Oprah Winfrey

Single Parents

When you have lemons ...
Making Lemonade

When you have lemons -
you make lemonade.
Create a new life...
that you never would trade.

You begin a new lifestyle
and hold down the fort.
Gather strength and great courage...
with single parent support.

A glass of water - that's your family
squeezed lemons - divorce
some sugar - is love
and ice - is the force.

The force keeps you strong
and encouraged with life.
You're now head of household...
no longer a wife.

Amazing what's accomplished
through times of great strife.
We learn of our power...
the foundation in life.

So when you have lemons
just make lemonade.
With single parent support
an extended family is made.

—Jodi Seidler, Single Parent Spokesperson
Creator of www.MakingLemonade.com, The Single Parent Network

CLIMB UP

She used to ask her Daddy
To pick her up on his shoulders bare
He would bend his large frame down to
Fling her little body high into the air

She would laugh out loud and
Give a great big squeal
I would watch in amazement
Wondering how this could really feel

He would carry her around for hours
And when the ride was through
She would come down
To share with me her incredible view

She would tell of seeing wonderful things
That seemed far away, shiny and new
She would tell me to get up on Daddy's shoulders
So that I could see them too

Now things have changed, as they often do
And Daddy is no longer around
So it appeared to me that her feet
Would forever be stuck to the ground

But that fate was not acceptable
Just because she had an absent father
So I told her to come on over here
Climb up on my shoulders daughter

I am not as tall in my frame
And when I pick you up it is with out the fling
But I have a dream and a vision for us
That can overcome anything

So climb up on my shoulders daughter
And take a look around
Climb up on my shoulders baby
Get those feet back off the ground

Climb up on my shoulders young lady
What do you see up there so high?
Climb up on my shoulders daughter
Let your fingertips brush the sky

And when the moment comes
After you have stood here for a while
Spread your wings and caught the air
Fly, fly my beautiful child

Climb up on my shoulders daughter
There is so much more to see
Climb up on my shoulders daughter
Be all you were created to be

— Trina-Leshay Williams —

Peanut Butter & Jelly Kisses

I skidded on a blueberry just the other day
stuck to the floor with honey, much to my dismay.
I've begged and I've pleaded and I think I sold my soul
just to get the little one to sit on the toilet bowl.

We say "goodnight" to everything in sight
only to do it again (sixteen more times) before the morning light.
Nothing like those Monday morning peanut butter and jelly kisses as
I'm walking out the door.
I am a single parent now, and forevermore.

Now I lay me down to sleep, I pray the Lord my job to keep
If I should die before I wake...
I pray the lord my "ex" to take.

And if I should wake before I die...
I want this oatmeal out of my eye.

— Marcella Brich —

Sisters

My daughter, Halihannah, 9 years old, was playing with her little
sister, 9 months old, last week and said, "Mom, I did not realize how
much I could love, until Kathy was born." She was present for the
birth and these two are well bonded.
—Patty Anderson, Mother of Two

Sisters touch your heart in ways no other could.
Sisters share... their hopes, their fears, their love, everything they
have. Real friendship springs from their special bonds.
—Carrie Bagwell

One's sister is a part of one's essential self,
an eternal presence of one's heart and soul and memory.
—Susan Cahill

Siblings are the people we practice on, the people who teach us about
fairness and cooperation and kindness and caring –
quite often the hard way.
—Pamela Dugdale

Every sister has a fund of embarrassing stories
she can bring out at the most effective moment.
—Pamela Dugdale

We are sisters. We will always be sisters.
Our differences may never go away, but neither, for me, will our song.
—Nancy Kelton, *My Sister: A Treasury of Companionship*

Sisters are connected throughout their lives by a special bond -
whether they try to ignore it or not. For better or for worse,
sisters remain sisters, until death do them part.
—Brigid McConville, from *Sisters: Love and Conflict Within
The Lifelong Bond*

Sisters is probably the most competitive relationship within the family, but once the sisters are grown, it becomes the strongest relationship.
—Margaret Mead

A sister can be seen as someone who is both ourselves and very much not ourselves - a special kind of double.
—Toni Morrison, Author

Sisters function as safety nets in a chaotic world simply by being there for each other.
—Carol Saline, from the TV series *Sisters*

What sets sisters apart from brothers and also from friends is a very intimate meshing of heart, soul and the mystical cords of memory.
—Carol Saline, from the TV series *Sisters*

For when three sisters love each other with such sincere affection, the one does not experience sorrow, pain, or affliction of any kind, but the other's heart wishes to relieve, and vibrates in tenderness... like a well-organized musical instrument.
—Elizabeth Shaw

Husbands come and go; children come and eventually they go. Friends grow up and move away. But the one thing that's never lost is your sister.
—Gail Sheeny, from the TV series *Sisters*

More than Santa Claus, your sister knows when you've been bad and good.
—Linda Sunshine

My sister taught me everything I need to know, and she was only in the sixth grade at the time.
—Linda Sunshine

Chance made us Sisters, hearts made us Friends.
—Unknown

So Glad You Choose Me

I'm So Glad You Chose Me

My dearest sweet one, my precious, amazing, radiant daughter,

You are my greatest gift, my joy, my teacher.
You are truly a rare treasure in my life and on this earth.
I want you to know how very honored I am to have been a part
of your journey to becoming the brilliant, loving, compassionate,
brave, pioneering woman that stands now before me.

I feel so very blessed that you chose me to be your mom.
You, my strong, wise, incredible daughter have taught me
more than you could ever possibly know.

You taught me how to speak what is in my heart, to love simply,
purely, honestly. Even with all the mistakes I made, the times I left
you feeling lost and alone because I was too caught up in me, you
rose up and found your way through.

You are such a gentle yet powerful spirit.
I love how you view things and I love the way you naturally teach
when you talk. Even when you were very young, I used to love to
listen to you talk to your friends as they asked you for advise.
You were always so loving, so wise beyond your years.
Thank you for allowing me to eavesdrop! You are amazing!

You are so genuine, so clear in your intent.
I am in constant awe of the way you care so deeply about the earth,
and all of it's creatures, always making your decisions with the
intention of the highest good of all concerned. You have taught me
how to connect with the world and with life in ways I would of never
had the opportunity to experience without you. I just love watching you
walk through life with the world at your command. The way you move
through life is magical! It is though I am watching a grandmother spirit.
I see you.

Your essence is tender, powerful, magnetic.
You radiate love and you are showered by love in return.

Your eyes sparkle with adventure, curiosity and wonder as you seek new ways to connect, understand, and live more intimately with the world around you. The animals and the children run to be near you, to be in your presence, to listen to your words of wisdom. I watch as everything seems to come to life as they feel you walk by. Your footsteps are grounded, purposeful, directed. With merely a smile and a wave of your hand the clouds parts, the grass grows and the flowers begin to bloom. There is a sacredness about you.

With powerful intent you use your voice to soothe and you heal with your feminine touch.

I am in constant awe of the woman before me.

You are love.

You are joy.

You are forever my role model and I hope to grow up to be just like you!

Most say that it is the mother that teaches the daughter, but I truly see that you are my teacher and I your humble student.

I love you, adore you and am forever grateful that you chose me to be your mom.

Thank you.

All my love,
XXXXXXXXXXXXXXOOOOOOOOOOOOOOO

Mom

—Catherine Tilley
Tribute dedicated to daughter Crystal Tilley

Sons

THROUGH OUR EYES
To my dear son on the day of your birth
Evan Bryce O'Brien Gregory

I look into your eyes my son,
and this is what I see,
I see the things that are to come,
and how these things may be.

To you we give all we can,
in health, and wealth, and love,
so that when these things that are to come,
they may be as good can be.

Some things good and some things bad
are going to come your way,
but if you use the sight we have,
we will help to guide your way.

Mistakes in life, we've made a few,
and learned of how they hurt,
and if you listen to our hearts,
we'll guide you to a good start.

We try to guide you in our way,
and hope it helps you see;
There are so many good things in life,
and these we hope will be.

The road you take in life, my son,
is really up to you.
All your mom and I can do,
is guide you as you run.

One thing we ask of you my son,
is to be kind to everyone.
And if you have a chance to help someone,
then guide them as they run.

© Copyright 1988. Reprinted with permission.
—Chris Gregory—

ANOTHER MOTHER FOR PEACE

New York City - June, 1967... Sometime between the 6-Day War between the Israelis and the Palestinians and June 22... the day my son, Marco, was born.

It was a sunny afternoon when my husband, Giovanni, and I decided to visit our friend, Enrico. A professional photographer, who had just returned from Vietnam, Enrico was in town for a couple of days, before taking off for his next assignment. He was working on a major project for *Life* Magazine - a cover, plus a 12 page spread with photographs of the war. With an assignment this significant, it is necessary to take hundreds, some times thousands of photos and then select the final few for publication.

Enrico was in the mist of sorting through the photos when we arrived at his apartment, and he began to tell us about how he was able to take such vivid and detailed photographs, even though many were extremely gruesome. It turns out that he had been given permission to fly on the rescue planes and helicopters which would swoop down, just long enough to pick up the wounded soldiers and then take off to the nearest medical facility or safe haven.

Standing there, nine months pregnant, I was not only shocked by the gruesome photos but also taken aback at the youth of the Americans and Vietnamese victims. They were the faces of young men, some barely past puberty, with peach hair on their faces... yet they were fighting a man's war. I couldn't help but wonder about the lives of the individuals. How did they end up fighting in this war? Where did they come from? What were their families like? What were their thoughts? What were their fears? Did they end up in these photos because they were just following orders? Did they really understand what they were fighting for?

As I thought about the anticipation and excitement I had been feeling, with the upcoming birth of my first child, I couldn't help but think about the mothers of these young men... Weren't they just as excited about the birth of their sons? Didn't they have dreams for them? Didn't they want a better life for them... an education, good health, success?   Were they going to be a part of the family business or strike out on their own, paving new frontiers? A wave of sadness came over me. One thing I knew for certain... none of these mothers brought their sons into the world with the idea of picking up a gun, or a grenade and killing someone else's son. I could not imagine bringing a son into the world, only to be sent to a far off land to kill others. You don't go through morning sickness, gaining weight, restless nights, sleep deprivation and labor, to then put them in harms way. This is not part of the maternal instinct.

Several days later, my son, Marco, was born. Everything was in tact... healthy, ten fingers and ten toes, and a sweetness that permeated my heart. What incredible joy is was becoming a mother!

The experience of viewing the photos of Vietnam were still very much with me. It was not something I could easily get out of my mind; I could never pretend that I never saw them. Instead, it became a call to action for me. One day while reading a magazine, I came across an article about a new organization that was in its start-up stage, *Another Mother for Peace.* Its motto is "War is Not Healthy for Children and Other Living Things."

I new it was calling out to me; I knew this was one small way that women could make their voices heard. I joined immediately and became an active member. The organization was active until 1979, the end of the Vietnam War, when it applied for an inactive status.

Fast forward to January, 2003 when I attended a conference, where Jean Shinoda Bolen, MD, was a guest speaker and author. She had just completed her seventh book, *The Millionth Circle: How to Change Ourselves and The World.* It was a call to "Gather the Women."

Unaware that Another Mother for Peace had been re-activated,* I heeded Jean's call, this time as a grandmother, and joined a circle in my city. It lasted for about nine months, before it folded due to dwindling numbers. Disappointed, I decided that the best thing I could do is to let go and see what tomorrow will bring. For me, it was a time of reflection and a time to regroup, however, something deep inside kept calling me to take action.

I realized that the bond of motherhood is a powerful connection for women of the world. Using it wisely has the potential to change the world.

—Judy Ranieri, MA, www.thewisdombox.com

*In 2003, with the threat of going to war with Iraq, the organization, *Another Mother for Peace* activated its status.
www.anothermotherforpeace.org

Mama, Mama

Mama, Mama, hold me tight,
Your little boy so small,
When I get into a fight,
Or scratch a knee or fall.

Mama, Mama, love me long
When I run to you.
Sing to me your pretty song,
Then I won't be blue.

Mama, Mama, you take the time
To listen to my fears,
And then, somehow, you magically
Dry up all my tears.

      Now,
Mama, Mama, a man am I,
And I must go away.
I must leave to fight a war
And I must leave today.

Mama, Mama, I'm so afraid.
The tears in my eyes burn,
For Mama, I must leave you now
And may never again return.

So, Mama, Mama, once again
Please do what you do best.
Hold me in your loving arms
And put my fears to rest.

—Connie Jameson

ALL SONS

The thing about a raising all boys is that it forces you to
accept that they are the way they are, in spite of your trying
to present them to the world as you imagined they would be.
It's a good lesson on looking at humanity.
—Linda Ferber

Sparkle - Tude Boosters

Today, we need little attitude "boosters" to help us overcome negative thoughts and actions that so easily creep into our daily lives. We were born with passion, a natural zest for life, curiosity, playfulness and grace. These "Sparkle-Tudes" help us rejuvenate that unbridled excitement, spirit, and joyful expression:

1) Start off the day on a positive tone.
How we wake up in the morning sets the pace for the rest of our day.

2) Have only positive thoughts toward yourself and others.
Guard carefully your thoughts . . . Attitude, or our truest belief about things, is that highly powered magnet that either attracts – or repels! Life is composed of our moment-by-moment thoughts.

3) Look for the good in yourself and others.
The Universal principle is that whatever thoughts we have about other people, these are also true of ourselves, as we are all connected, and we are all one. What we see in others are reflections of ourselves.

4) Believe in yourself, your talents, and your unique gifts.
You were given significant strengths, and have developed skills to support those – use them!

5) Don't to take things "personally." Let it go and move on!

6) Affirm a spirit of gratitude throughout the day.
Start off the day with positive affirmations and anticipations of the day. I say, "Thank you God, for the gift of this glorious day. I rise, rejoice and am glad in it. Thank you for every way in which I experience your love. I give thanks that my every thought, word and act is only loving and supportive." End the day summarizing all the blessings you received

7) Utilize these unconditional support systems to keep your balance, perspective and sanity: Pets; Faith; Passion Hobbies; and Special People.

— Sheryl Roush, Speaker, Author *Sparkle-Tudes!*, *Heart of A Woman*, and contributing author to *The Princess Principle: Women Helping Women Discover Their Royal Spirit*, 18 inspirational stories
www.SparklePresentations.com

Stay at Home Moms

You Can Have It All

1. MAKE THE MOST OF YOUR LIFE EXPERIENCES. No matter what happens in your life, grow from those experiences. Don't allow difficult situations to diminish you or your dreams.

2. CHOOSE A PRIMARY FOCUS FOR EACH STAGE OF YOUR LIFE AND BE INTENSELY COMMITTED TO IT. A primary focus gives you a FRAME for the way you approach the world.

3. NO MATTER WHAT YOUR PRIMARY FOCUS IS, ALWAYS MAKE SURE THAT YOU ARE IN SOME WAY KEEPING YOUR PROFESSIONAL SKILLS ALIVE.
Read current writings in your field, rent tapes from the library, talk to others periodically who are still working full-time in your area of expertise, attend conferences and workshops, go back to school part time if you possibly can.

4. RE-EVALUATE YOUR PRIORITIES AT LEAST ONCE A YEAR, ALWAYS KEEPING THE LONG TERM IN MIND. When the time is right to change priorities and focus, communicate that clearly to others and make decisions that support that change.

5. BE CREATIVE.   Whatever your life situation may be, do the very best you can within the focus you've chosen.

6. NETWORK CONSTANTLY. Get to know people in your community, your church, schools. Let your skills and talents be known by others. Then, when your focus changes, you will already have a group of people who can recommend you.

7. BELIEVE IN YOURSELF AND YOUR DREAMS. Even though you may have chosen to put your career "on the back burner" for a while, always approach each life task or experience like a professional.

—Barbara A. Glanz, Speaker, Consultant, Work/Life Balance Expert Author *CARE Packages for the Home—Dozens of Ways to Regenerate Spirit Where You Live* and   *Balancing Acts: More Than 250 Guilt-free, Creative Ideas to Blend your Work and your Life*
www.BarbaraGlanz.com

Staying Authentic

Authentic: Worthy of trust, reliance, or belief; genuine.

We are a unique representation of Spirit.
Allowing our authentic self to shine forth lights the way for Spirit's essence to express in this world.
—Debbie Barnett, Speaker, www.DebbieBarnett.com

Why compare yourself with others?
No one is the entire world can do a better job of being you than you.
—Susan Carlson

There is nothing meaningful in life than honoring your authentic self—your true nature—and expressing it in the world. You are allowing your Light to shine and touch the world...the truth in your heart and soul. It's allowing yourself to be guided by Divine Truth and Wisdom, each and every day, and doing your Highest, most authentic work in the world. It's joyfully creating and living your Highest purpose! It's following your heart's wisdom, and being real in every sense.
—Valerie Rickel, Founder and Soul, www.SoulfulLiving.com

If you're someone who's been living everyone else's life other than your own, it's never too late to awaken your Authentic Self and listen closely as the truth is whispered to you. This takes some courage. It means being willing to say no when you might normally say yes and the yes isn't authentic. You may realize your truth is wanting a more simple life, one that doesn't have to keep up with the Jones'.
Whatever it is for you, be willing to create some personal time so you can get reacquainted with your Self and start to live your life. Allow yourself to be selfish.
—Linda Salazar, Certified Personal Life Coach, Author, Speaker www.AwakenTheGenieWithin.com

Our childlike self is the deepest level of our being.
—Marianne Williamson, Speaker, Author *Return to Love*

We can't become what we need to be by remaining what we are.
—Oprah Winfrey

Teenagers

WHAT EVERY TEENAGE GIRL NEEDS:

A tender shoulder to cry on.
A best friend to confide in.
A mom who listens to her.
A committed teacher.
A warm bed.
A cozy home.
A bedroom she can decorate any way she wants to.
A group she belongs to.
A set of friend who accepts her.
A powerful dream for her future.
A personal cheerleader to encourage her.
A confidante who says, "I know, I understand, and I care."
A mentor.
A strong belief in herself.
A positive way to express her creativity.
A vision for her life that excites her.
A goal that fuels her.
A hobby she excels in.
A constructive way to blow off her teenage stress .
A dad who makes her feel loved and special .
A family who allows her to be herself.
A puppy to love.
A boyfriend who treats her like a queen.
A desire to help another.
A reminder that the teenage years are temporary.
AND...
A deep knowing she is lovable and "PERFECT"
exactly the way God made her.

—Tami Walsh, M.A., President, Teen Coach
Speaker, Author *The Did Wells Journal* for teen girls, and top-selling
audio CD for parents entitled, *Communication: Turning Battles Into
Bridges With Your Teenager.*

Resources for raising teens today, www.TeenWisdom.Com

Never lend your car to anyone to whom you have given birth.
—Erma Bombeck

The young always have the same problem - how to rebel and conform at the same time. They have now solved this by defying their parents and copying one another.
—Quentin Crisp

When I was a teenager, I recall struggling with my identity and my self-worth. There were many times that I came home and cried on my bed. Boys made fun of me, and called me names. There were numerous times I felt ugly and worthless. I will never forget the gift of you! The beautiful words you shared with me. You kept telling me not to pay attention to such nonsense, and how beautiful and special I was. You forever gave me strength, love, courage and passion. Your support and love are in my heart forever. I love forever, with every fiber of my being.
—Lisa R. Delman, Speaker, Author *Dear Mom, I've Always Wanted You To Know,* Daughters Share Letters from the Heart (book and play) www.TheHeartProject.com

People change and forget to tell each other.
—Lillian Hellman

Remember, we all stumble, every one of us.
That's why it's a comfort to go hand in hand.
—Emily Kimbrough

Few things are more satisfying than seeing your children
have teenagers of their own.
—Doug Larson

The best way to keep children at home is to make the home atmosphere pleasant, and let the air out of the tires.
—Dorothy Parker

Heredity is what sets the parents of a teenager
wondering about each other.
—Laurence J. Peter

Teenagers complain there's nothing to do,
then stay out all night doing it.
—Bob Phillips

I never expected to see the day when girls would get sunburned
in the places they do now.
—Will Rogers

Adolescence is perhaps nature's way of preparing parents
to welcome the empty nest.
—Karen Savage and Patricia Adams, *The Good Stepmother*

The average teenager still has all the faults his parents outgrew.
—Unknown

ADVICE ABOUT LOVE

Wait for the boy who pursues you, the one who will make an
ordinary moment seem magical, the kind of boy who brings out the
best in you and makes you want to be a better person.
Wait for the boy who will be your best friend.
Wait for the boy who makes you smile like no other boy makes you
smile and when he smiles you know he needs you.
Wait for the boy who wants to show you off the the world
when you are in sweats and have no makeup on, but appreciates it
when you get all dolled up for him.
And most of all wait for the boy who will put you at the center of his
universe, because obviously he's at the center of yours.

—Mandi Nowlin, Age 21, daughter and sister

OUTSIDE LOOKING IN

Everyone is on the outside looking in.
They all judge too quickly
not knowing what has been.

It makes me crazy because they don't know how I feel.
They just say all the things that bug me
and don't even know what's real.

I don't know why I let it get so far under my skin.
I have too many insecurities,
not enough faith to lift my chin.

The past is the past and there's nothing I can do.
I think I'm sure but then someone says something
about what I think is true.

I guess I'll just deal with comments,
get through and continue to stride.
But insanity builds when people talk that aren't on the inside.

— Erika Enggren —
Age 15

CONTROL

Dear Mom,

Please don't try to teach me, more than you can love me.
Don't try to save me, more than you can let me be.

Don't try to push me away more than you can keep me near.
Don't try to scare me just because you feel fear.

Don't try to take from me so that I will continue to give.
And please stop hurting me, 'cause it's your pain that you live.

Make love the most important thing you do.
It's all I've ever needed from you.

Your loving daughter
—Name withheld by request

THE GIRL IN THE GLASS

When you get what you want in your struggle for Self,
And the world makes you Queen for A Day,
Just go to the mirror and look at yourself,
And see what that girl has to say.

For it isn't your father or mother or brother
whose judgment upon you must pass;
The person whose verdict means most in your life
Is the girl staring back from the glass.

She's the girl you must please, never mind all the rest,
for she's with you clear to the end;
And you've passed your most difficult,
dangerous test.

If the girl in the glass is your friend.
You may fool the whole world down the pathway of years,
And get pats on the back as you pass;
But your final reward will be heartache and tears,
If you cheated the girl in the glass

— Author Unknown —

Recommended Reading List for Parents:
As you navigate through the adolescent years here are some books
with invaluable information to help you see into your teen's world.

A Good Enough Parent, Bruno Bettelheim (instinctive childrearing)
Adolescence, Miller Newton
A Tribe Apart, Patricia Hersch (teen issues as they mature)
Childhood In America, Paula Fass, Maryann Mason
Girls on The Verge, Vendela Vida (rituals to create their identity)
In A Different Voice, Carol Gilligan (girls' developmental stages)
My Mother, Myself, Ann Friday
Odd Girl Out:The Hidden Culture of Aggression in Girls-
Parent Effectiveness Training, Gordon (handbook of techniques)
Sex and Sensibility—A Parent's Guide to Talking Sense About Sex
Debra Rottman (addresses both moral/physical issues of sexuality)
The Romance of Risk, Lynn Ponton (extreme cases risky behaviors)
The Field Guide To the American Teenager, DiPrisco and Riera
Uncommon Sense For Parents, Michael Riera (high school and life)

—Tami Walsh, M.A., Teen Coach, www.TeenWisdom.com

The Dress

This was my first year away at college, and my first college dance. I had grown up with my mom making most of my best clothes. I never made it simple, though, as I would pick the collar from one pattern, the sleeves from another and the torso of the dress from yet another pattern. We had picked the most beautiful shiny shocking pink brocade fabric and rhinestone buttons. It was to be a short A-line dress, short sleeves, mandarin collar with buttons down the front. I lived an hour away from parents, so fittings took place on the week-ends when I could get home.

Finally, the week had arrived for both the completion of the dress and the dance. After returning from my parent's home to my apartment with my new creation, I proudly hung the dress, covered in a blue plastic cleaners bag, in my living room where I could see it on the wall heater. I then went to class with thoughts of the coming weekend in my head. Upon arriving back at my apartment, I noticed a definite odor. It smelled like someone had burnt toast or maybe a dress. OH MY GOD, my gorgeous original dress now had a blue plastic bag melted to the back of it with burnt grid marks from the heater.

I called my mom hysterical–and unable to speak. She was so scared about what might be wrong. When I could finally get the words out, I told her about burning my dress. She calmly told me to go back to the fabric store, buy a yard of the pink brocade, bring that and the smoldering dress to her. Sniveling, I did as I was told.

Two days before the dance, I was back in my home town watching my mother tear my beautiful pink dress apart and replacing the back panel to look as good as new. I then drove back to college and went to the dance with only a speck of a burnt mark still showing at the back hem of the dress. I was a happy co-ed. I later wore that dress on my twenty-first birthday on a blind date with my future husband.

My mother has saved my life in so many ways and still does today at eighty-five years old. She is a special woman who taught me the selflessness of being a mother. Motherhood has been the greatest thing I have ever done and that is because I had the perfect example.

—Linda Lev, Karen Robertson's (much younger) sister
In tribute to memories I have of our mother, Garnet Brassfield

Through the Eyes of Children

My daughter Rose, two years old, and I sleep in the same bed and recently I have been witnessing some pretty unusual and interesting interactions between her and what I think are her angels. I like to listen to the soundtrack, "In Search of Angels" before bed. It always gives me chills and I think the angels like it.

One night my daughter jumps up in bed in the dark, and starts singing along, but her eyes swam back and forth in the dark and she was laughing, like she was watching something flying. I got quiet and watched her for a while. She had her head tilted back and was making like little dog paddling swimming motions (something she had never done before), twirling her arms around in circles making little flying motions with her hands. I asked, "Are you seeing angels?" She grinned from ear to ear and nodded her head. "Where are the angels?" She pointed to the ceiling, "Up high." I asked her, "What do the angels do?" She just grinned and made more paddling motions with her arms. I took her to a bookstore, showed her an angel art book. She didn't respond, until we got to a picture of Mary surrounded by flying cherubs, then she shrieked, "Angels!"

She has seen a picture of the Virgin Mary's face and shrieked "Angel!" I don't know if she has seen her before or not, or mistook her for an angel. I also heard her talking in the dark for a long time.

I don't question these incidents, but I do find them comforting.

I believe children often see things adults don't see. It reminds me of the only time I have ever seen anything myself. Once when I was very young, I was scared to sleep and I prayed for my angels to be with me. I slept with the light on. When I woke up, I saw golden hair quivering just over the edge of my bed. My eyes were wide open, and I wasn't dreaming. I leaned over the side of the bed and saw a child about 3 foot tall, looking away from me. It turned around and looked at me, it had a cherubim face and blue eyes. I don't recall wings. In a second it was gone. I wonder if that was an angel. When my daughter does these things I wonder if she is seeing an angel like I saw when I was very young.

—Chrissy Hurley

Time Management

Time management seems to be the most important element in a single parent household (or any household for that matter). As single parents, it seems we never have enough time in the day to do ALL we need to do for ourselves and for our family.

Time is a commodity, and we have to learn to use it wisely. We can learn to budget our time just as we budget our finances. Here are some tips to help manage your busy single parent world, and create a sense of organization in your life. Departmentalize and add more structure to bring together your days. It may amaze you that you actually CAN create some time just for you...

Make lists, don't rely on your mind (or what's left of it) to remember what things need to be done and when. Whatever you haven't gotten accomplished today, move it over to tomorrow's list. Place the urgent and the most challenging to do's on the top of tomorrow's list.

Pay bills all at one time and put a little yellow sticky memo on the piles that need to be mailed mid-month or at the end of month. This way you only have to get stressed out one day a month and your bills get mailed out on time.

Get an engagement calendar for play dates or custody arrangements, homework, meetings, bills, personal and school events. Take the pressure off your memory skills and keep track of events and appointments on paper. Keep your mind freed up from the strain of having to remember everything you're juggling. A side benefit is that you'll discover excess energy and a more focused attention span.

Keep a notepad by your phone or bed to jot down things as they come to mind. This is a great tool so that you don't forget those fleeting thoughts or morning reminders upon awakening. You can also keep a small tape recorder in the car, so you don't miss a thought or reminder driving (especially because we spend so much time in the car). Just drive carefully and watch out for those drivers on cellular phones.

Choose a day or night that you will do your grocery shopping and errand running each week. Choose a consistent day to clean your home. Stick to your schedule and forget about these responsibilities the rest of the week.

Buy things in bulk (save time and money) and if needed, split these purchases with another single parent or neighbor. Now that we have places like Smart & Final, Sam's Club and Costco, it makes it easier to buy in bulk, save money and always have what we need on hand.

Teach your child how to make his or her breakfast, help with dishes and laundry (make a game of it), empty the dishwasher and clean his/her room. Make a 'chores chart' and place a star on the chart for these accomplishments. (I get creative and use carnival tickets for my nine-year-old...and he receives a special prize when those tickets reach a certain quantity.)

Maximize your trips. Create a flow chart in your head of where you have to drive... and target those chores by their location. Don't run around all over town to get errands done; do them by area and by priority. Call a store to see if they have an item in stock... save yourself a trip, and some time. If you have a friend going to a grocery store... have them pick up a few items for you.

Think Smart, save time. Review your priorities and change those things that aren't working. Get up earlier or go to bed later to get things done that can't be done during the day, or designate a weekend while your child is with the other parent or has a play date, to accomplish what's needed.

Read at least 10 minutes a night to unwind. If your child is old enough, you can designate a 10 or 15 minute reading time, where you both read your separate books together. And, why not make it a cozy time by snuggling with your child while you read together!

Remember not to cling to worn out ways of scheduling your time if they no longer work for you. As we evolve and our lifestyle changes, we have to modify the way we spend our time doing errands, housework, bill paying, scheduling appointments and making the most of every hour in the day. Why not speak to other single parents, or people you admire, to find out what has worked for them in the realm of budgeting time?

Most importantly, don't forget to take time out for yourself. As much as our children are our gifts, we are theirs as well. We are their role models, teaching them by example - so be a great example. Prioritize, replenish yourself and think smart....it all begins with you!

—© Jodi Seidler, Single Parent Spokesperson
Creator of www.MakingLemonade.com, The Single Parent Network.

To My Child

I wish that I could save you
from the struggles and the strife,
and all the disappointments
you'll encounter in your life.

But if I did I'd rob you
of the chance for you to know
the strong, determined person
into whom I hope you'll grow.

For if you never stumble
you will always fear to fall,
not knowing you possess the strength
to overcome it all.

And if you always win,
then you will not know how to lose.
And if you never make a choice,
you'll always fear to choose.

It's through these lessons in our lives
we learn which paths to take.
So don't be paralyzed by fear
that you will make mistakes.

Have faith that you can stand alone
and know that I'll be near,
to help and guide you as you grow
throughout the coming years.

— Sandy Holman McVey —

Dedicated to Cooper Dean,
whose birth on 1/11/04 inspired this poem.

Tranquili-Tea

Tea Prayer

Be still and know God.
Be still and know God is all there is.
I claim in quiet, peaceful tranquility
that I am one with God.
My strength and satiation
comes from within.

I go there often to drink of the tranquil waters.
I am refreshed, replenished and rejuvenated.
From this place of purity,
I drink of my own goodness
and know my vessel will never empty.

My needs are satisfied,
my desires realized.
I am awakened and heightened.
No more need I be frightened.
I am all I need to be.

Here, in tranquility, free from hostility
and perceived reality,
I remember my divinity.
Thank you, Tranquil One.
With my breath, I let it be.
I allow this peaceful Force to set me free.
And so It does, and so It is, and so I am.

Amen

—Darlene Fahl-Brittian—
Certified Tea Specialist
Sipping Tea - Celebrating Me
www.TakeUpTheCup.com

Two Separate Souls

Mother & Daughter: The Coming Together of Two Souls

Two separate souls, two entirely different reality experiences.

One inward, and one outward,
  Dancing around where neither is, like two planets
  barely missing collision.
  Each energy field repelling the other.

  Coming together only in a hope of a common reality,
  seemingly doomed to a separateness of heart.

But a stream, a thread, barely noticeable, buried under illusion,
  but nonetheless vital and true,
    emerged now and again,
      nurtured by a mother's love.
        Breaking past barriers that created distances
        measured by universes.
  Her generosity that seeps past the illusion—
Awakens their hearts, which holds the truth, connecting the souls,
beyond sense.

As one mellows and barriers dissolve,
  And the other matures, and enters upon equal ground.
    My heart expands in gratitude.

That you are my mother and I am the daughter born of you.

—Jane Ilene Cohen, Transformational and Intuitive Counselor, specializing in relationships, www.janecohen.net

© 2004 Jane Ilene Cohen   Reprinted with permission.

Unconditional Support

4 Simple Ways to Nurture Yourself and Keep Your Sanity

Here are four simple ways to help keep balance in your daily life, so you are able to be there for yourself, your children, and loved ones.

According to stress management experts, we have four support systems available that offer us unconditional love and support.

1) Pets
Pets are nonjudgmental, forgiving, sensitive and supportive. They instinctively KNOW when we need a hug or are feeling emotional, depressed and upset, and don't run at the first sign of tears! Medical research even proves that hugging a pet lowers blood pressure, and helps to rebuild the immune system.

2) Faith – Spiritual Belief System
This inner compass enables us bring forth that wisdom, authenticity and insight into all we do on a daily basis. These beliefs center our moral foundation, offering direction, and trust to walk to our path in this world.

3) Passion Hobbies
Passion Hobbies are pastimes that nurture our spirit and balance our lives. Reading; walking, dancing, running, aerobics or exercise; crafts; puzzles; playing with kids; or shopping!

4) Special People
These may be relatives, or significant others, still be living, or have already made their transition. Highly supportive kindred spirits. We can pick up conversations with them, right where we left off, without missing a beat.

You have numerous gifts to give to the world today — and those gifts are needed. Nurture yourself first, and those challenges become easier to handle, with less stress, greater peace and calm. Utilize these unconditional support systems to bring you more balance and joy in your daily life.

—Sheryl Roush, Speaker, Author *Sparkle-Tudes!* Book Series
www.SparklePresentations.com

Values

Shared What You Have

For a marriage to last 60 or so years, they both had benevolent spirits but not many possessions. During the depression, men would come to back door of our home in Austin asking if we had any odd jobs they could do. Mother always believed in helping people maintain their dignity. So before she gave them Vegetable soup and big slice of corn bread, in exchange they sharpened Dad's knives which were still warm from the last bowl of soup and sharpening. Mother managed and Daddy let her. It worked for them.
—Morgie Peirano

You demonstrate your values and beliefs daily by the way
you live your life.
—Lynn Pierce, Author *Change One Thing, Change Your Life*

If you don't set a baseline standard for what you'll accept in life,
you'll find it's easy to slip into behaviors and attitudes or a quality
of life that's far below what you deserve.
—Anthony Robbins, Author

What is important is simple:
Know what you value and invest your time accordingly.
This is integrity and it will bring you peace.
—Rhoberta Shaler, PhD

We can tell our values by looking at our checkbook stubs.
—Gloria Steinem

Welcome Child

Christening Ceremony

Charles Dickens, the British writer wrote "Every baby born into this world is a finer one than the one before." He was, of course, perfectly correct and he didn't even know my grandson. If he had met, this beautiful addition to the world, he might have written a book about him. After all, many books are written about a baby's love.

Today this child is being christened, and getting a very special blessing from God and those here today that are offering their love and guidance on this spiritual journey throughout his lifetime.

He is a new little seed that will grow only when nurtured by those who love him. His quest to live a good and wholesome life will come from his parents, as well as family and friends.

I feel so blessed that my daughter choose me and her father to give her life. Now she and her husband have been blessed with a gift from God... this child, whose soul has selected them to instill inner spiritual qualities of love, joy, creativity and kindness.

Babies are all about new beginnings and they are about confidence, hope, faith, trust in the future. Babies are truly a cause for celebration. I think a baby is the best kind of prayer there is. Just look at their innocence and you will know why so many people believe that they are a little bit of Heaven here on Earth. Now mind you, they are very human. This means that they require 24 hour catering. Babies dribble, they dirty their diapers and they howl—usually to be fed and loved.

May God bless and watch over this child... every step of your life. To the parents, I wish you a love filled life together and with my first grandson. Happy First Mother's Day to you. This is one of many you will be celebrating.

Last but not least, I vow to spoil my grandchild every chance I get!

—Beverly Weurding

Dedicated to Dominic Conrad Huss, Christened on Mother's Day, Sunday, May 14, 2006

We're Goin' to College!

What do you say to a daughter who is turned down by the college of her choice and won't take "no" for an answer – five times!

Meet Heather Brittany, a vivacious seventeen-year-old high school senior who believes in herself and all her possibilities. At age four, she endured arduous surgery to save her life. Her mom, who spent two weeks camping by her bedside, called it "our special adventure," and indeed it secured a mother/daughter bond that has not been broken.

Heather decided then and there that when she went off to college, she would take along Mommy and Halloween, her cat. By age seven, Heather was diagnosed with severe learning disabilities and placed in a special program. Instead of viewing herself as challenged, she chose to see herself as a "special star." Although she struggled with her studies, she excelled in athletics, drama, and her work with animals.

By eighth grade, Heather was a straight "A" student, assisting other learning-disabled children to overcome their obstacles. Then, much to her apprehensive delight, the school administrators disqualified Heather from the special resource program and returned her to regular classes. She knew that high school would offer numerous challenges, and she was right. She soon faltered. Her grades fell to "C's" and "D's" because she couldn't master the art of test taking. She pleaded for re-admittance to the learning-disabled program, but her application was denied. She was told that she needed to fail completely to qualify!

Failure is not part of Heather's vocabulary, so she sought outside help. College admission was foremost in her mind. She had to work harder than all her friends, but she was determined to get top grades while remaining involved in the many activities she felt were important to being a well-rounded individual. Her hours were filled with leadership responsibilities, including the 4-H club, church, charities, her menagerie of adopted animals, and volunteer work. She also scheduled weekly "tea times" with her mom who was her constant cheerleader and motivator. They pasted positive quotations on the walls of her bedroom to inspire her to greatness, and together they visited college campuses so Heather could review her future options.

Heather fell in love with San Diego State University in California. By her senior year, her high school grade point average was a solid 3.5. She was confident she would be accepted. Instead, she got a rejection letter. Rejection number one. She immediately phoned the Admissions Office to ask about the appeal process. "This year there is no appeal process," she was told. "We had 45,000 applications for 5,000 slots. We're sorry, but we can forward your application to another school." Rejection number two.

But Heather didn't want another school. Her dream was SDSU, and her mom had encouraged her to imagine her reality, reach for the stars, and expect to land on them. Heather reasoned that the school just didn't understand her potential or know her as a person. There was no way she was giving up now. She looked at the quotations she lived by plastered on her bedroom walls. She could write memorable essays, create outstanding projects, and perform at the highest levels in verbal examinations, although she had not mastered taking tests in school. Now she was confronting the biggest test of all.

"Never, never, never give up," Winston Churchill had said. "We must either find a way, or make one" said Hannibal when he crossed the uncrossable Alps. Heather was determined to design her own future. But how?

She put together a formal appeal to the Admissions Office. She gathered her most recent school transcripts and got even more glowing letters of recommendation from her teachers, counselors, talent agent, principal, and community leaders. So many letters arrived that they couldn't all be submitted. Then she made a video highlighting her acting and communication skills. This impressive PR package was sent off to the Admissions Office. Again, Heather was confident that this time they'd "see Heather, the person, not just a number." Acceptance was just days away.

When a reply arrived from SDSU, she eagerly tore open the envelope. It was a duplicate of her first rejection letter. Rejection number three.

Most kids would have given up. Not Heather! Rejection was nothing new. After all, she had been acting and modeling in TV and film since she was a baby. Instead of "being sensible," she picked up the phone and called the Admissions Office again. A special orientation day was approaching for admitted students, and she wanted to attend. "The event is only for our admitted freshman," she was told. "I'm sorry, but you are not one of them." Rejection number four.

So did Heather finally give up? Remember, this is the young woman who had coined the motto: "Tell me 'no,' then watch me go!" Heather kept talking and talking, using all her best communication and persuasion skills. Finally, the Administration Office wearily said she would not be barred if she showed up.

With her mother in tow, Heather traveled to San Diego and introduced herself and her situation to everyone she met. She persuaded faculty members to support her and endorse her efforts. Her persistence and determination in the face of defeat was spectacular. After her journey, she followed up with thank-you notes, e-mails, and personal calls to everyone she had met.

Another SDSU letter arrived. Again, she had been denied. Rejection number five! Surely any sensible person would have acknowledged defeat.

Not Heather. She immediately contacted the Chair of her declared major and asked for help. By this time, the Department of Theatre had recognized her unquenchable enthusiasm and sense of purpose, traits essential for success in the entertainment world. They decided to recruit her. They supported her admissions appeal and assured the University that they would be responsible for tracking her progress, mentoring her, and helping her exceed the University's standards. Heather had found her champion.

On April 15, 2002, Heather opened the envelope containing her latest high school grades. She now had a 3.67 grade point average, plus numerous outstanding teenager awards. Still, she had received no college admittance letter. At last, her vision started to waiver. "Mom, I have total faith that I deserve to be a student at SDSU. I know I will add value to their campus, but I'm getting discouraged."

"Honey," her mother responded, "keep daring to dream. Like our friend Dr. Bernie Siegel says, 'hoping means seeing that the outcome you want is possible, then working for it.' Persevere. Pray. Persist. No matter what happens, you are already a star." Together they prayed, they laughed, and then they played.

At 2 PM on April 16, the phone rang. "She's ours! She is all ours!" screamed an excited voice.

The co-chair of the Department of Theatre had just been notified that Heather was finally accepted by SDSU and into the Department of Theatre, the most crowded department on campus.

It took more than an hour to get the news to Heather who was still at school. Her mother finally reached her by phone. "Heather, you did it! You're in!" They both shouted and cried together.

Heather responded, "No, Mom, we did it! We're going to college!"

Heather was rejected five times in forty-five days.
Any sensible person would have given up. Not Heather.
She was tenacious, determined, and passionate about her abilities.
She never lost sight of her dream. And, of course, she had a mother who supported her in her decisions.

This is going to be the best Mother's Day ever because next fall Heather and I are going to college.

© 2002 Cynthia Brian. Reprinted with permission.
http://www.star-style.com
http://www.goddessgals.com

Editor's notes:
Heather was on her first set at 3 days old. Her accolades today include national commercials, graced the covers of magazines, had the privilege of slapping actor Hugh Grant, doing cartwheels with comedian Robin Williams, appeared on *Veronica Mars*, and *See Arnold Run* (a look at the life of Arnold Schwarzenegger, from his early days as a body builder up until his successful campaign for Governor of California).

Currently, Cynthia Brian and Heather Brittany are the charismatic mother/daughter dynamos known as The Stella Donne Goddess Gals, working together in films, television, radio, commercials, print, and numerous speaking/writing endeavors. Their nationally syndicated upbeat radio show, Starstyle®-Be the Star You Are! may be found at http://www.worldtalkradio.com/show.asp?sid=118

Woman

A woman is a wondrous, magnificent creature,
a princess a goddess, a queen.
She is worthy of, and deserves,
love, adoration and respect.
She is a mystical creature
blessed and guided by an inner knowing
of what is right and true.
She gives life and nurtures it ever so gently
with tenderness and love.
Her spirit is playful and passionate,
Her movement fluid and graceful.
Her strength lies in her knowledge of self
as she moves forward freely, confidently,
caressing life with gentleness and greatness.
Allowing love to flood her heart,
she heals with her feminine touch
and give birth to things divine
She speaks not in anger but centers herself in truth
and uses the power of her voice to soothe,
speaking calmly, clearly, compassionately
for the highest good of all concerned.
She is magnetic, regal and wise.
She carries her head held high.
She has an inner light, a spiritual essence
that, when revealed,
is so enchanting, so captivating, so alluring
that all who experience, this vision of loveliness,
find that they are drawn to her
with the intense desire to know
her secrets of beauty, wisdom and peace.

— Catherine Tilley —

A Woman

Be very careful if you make a woman cry,
because God counts her tears.
The woman came out of a man's rib.
Not from his feet to be walked on.
Not from his head to be superior, but from the side to be equal.
Under the arm to be protected,
and next to the heart to be loved.

— The Talmud —

You start out happy that you have no hips or boobs.
All of a sudden you get them, and it feels sloppy.
Then just when you start liking them, they start drooping.
—Cindy Crawford

One is not born a woman, one becomes one.
—Simone de Beauvoir, *The Second Sex,* 1949

A woman's whole life is a history of the affections.
—Washington Irving

God made man, and then He said, "I can do better than that,"
and made women.
—Adela Rogers St. Johns

Sure God created man before woman.
But then you always make a rough draft before the final masterpiece.
—Unknown

Women in Religion

The Historical Mary Magdalene

The false image of Mary Magdalene as a penitent sinner saved by Jesus cannot be found in the Gospels of the New Testament. It is a product of rumor and innuendo that resulted from a sermon given by Pope Gregory in the sixth century when he combined the figures of Mary Magdalene, Mary of Bethany and the "sinful woman" found in Luke's Gospel. Even though it is entirely false, this sexually charged slander against Mary Magdalene has persisted for fourteen centuries, and has been the basis for how Mary Magdalene is often portrayed in modern media.

The Gospels of the New Testament are very clear about who Mary Magdalene was: She was a prominent disciple of Jesus who witnessed his crucifixion after all the male disciples had fled in fear for their own lives. After his death, Mary Magdalene was the first disciple to receive an appearance of the risen Jesus. She was then commissioned, either by an angel or by Jesus himself, to communicate her experience to the other disciples. Since no male disciple had a vision of the risen Jesus until after Mary convinced them that her own experience was valid, Christianity itself would never have begun were it not for the woman from Magdala.

–Sharon Hooper, Coach, Retreat Facilitator
Author, *The Wisdom of Mary Magdalene*, 36 teachings card deck
www.MaryMagdaleneCards.com

Editor's note:
Sharon's husband, Richard Hooper, M.Div., a former Lutheran pastor, and author of *The Crucifixion of Mary Magdalene: the Historical Tradition of the First Apostle and the Ancient Church's Campaign to Suppress It*

The Mother of Moses and Her Legacy

Knowing her son would almost certainly be killed, the mother of
Moses (her name is known as **Jochebed**) put her newborn son in a
raft and cast him adrift in the river. Whether you are Jewish, Muslim,
Christian, or an avid movie fan, the rest of the story is, as they say,
history. Mothers take great risks and sacrifice for their children.

And this is true of surrogate mothers, as well. There are many
stories of animals who succor the young of others. The young grow
up not knowing another mother and so it is. Mom is where you get
nourished. Mom is who keeps you warm at night. Mom is who brings
you back from the brink of disaster.

I have often thought of mothers who adopt as generally brave souls.
My friend, Gail, for example, has adopted three children. She, like the
Pharaoh's daughter, found small, vulnerable and needy bodies in a
foreign stream and added love. She brought them into her home and,
with the help of her biological daughter, has helped them forget (to a
great degree) that they did, indeed, have another life long ago.

I know other women who have adopted, have taken babies from the
bulrushes and they are no less proud of them than if they had given
birth, themselves.

The women who give up their biological children in the hopes that
the child will find a better life, are just as courageous. Certainly in
the face of death, giving up the child is an act of ultimate love, as
the Biblical story of Solomon reinforces. But when life is uncertain,
when certain death is not the outcome, and when you know you
can't or won't be a gift to the child, isn't giving the child up just
as courageous?

Motherhood is about heart and a great heart is a wondrous thing.
In celebrating mothers, there are those who choose the pain and joy
of childbirth and those who embrace the child much later. And
when the child is loved, s/he cares not. Looking back to antiquity
or forward to a world yet unknown, mothers are here for keeps.
And aren't we just the lucky ones?

—John Reddish

Words Cannot Express

My mom raised me and my sister by herself and did the job of two parents. She knew in her infinite wisdom what took to be kind, supportive, and often employed tough love for our own good. One year, while we were still kids, my sister and I gave my mother a Father's Day card. What started out as a cute joke, became one of my mom's most proud and cherished moments.

Things I heard from my mother all throughout my upbringing:
"Independence and self-reliance are the greatest gifts any parent can give their child."

"Parenting is not a popularity contest. Occasionally I will make decisions you might not appreciate at the moment, but I can deal with that because I know in my heart I am doing right by you."

"If I have a choice between me being unhappy and you being unhappy, better you be unhappy."

"One day when you're an adult, you'll look back and thank me."

"Learn a little bit about everything. About music and art, writing and poetry. The worst you could be in life is an educated bum."

Mom taught me:
Success doesn't always mean first place or a gold medal. It can mean just having the courage to face your fears, just having the courage to try. (It certainly helped me deal with disappointment and failure, and put them in a healthy perspective.)

My mother always rationalized with her tough ways, "The greatest gifts that any parent can give their children is independence and self-reliance." Then, in 1983 when I left New York for San Diego to train for the Olympics in the Decathlon, my mom told me the thing she was most proud of, my independence and self-reliance, was also the thing that broke her heart because it took me so far away from her.

—James Bachelor
Dedicated to Rochelle Bachelor

Working Miracles

My Mother, The Miracle Worker

Mom was small, but mighty, and her footsteps were distinctive. She always walked in double time, as if she never had enough hours to do everything she was put on this earth to do. To hear her softly hum and sing as she went about her housework, one would think that she had not a problem in the world, she carried them all with such grace.

As a young wife and mother of two tiny babies, she took on a huge new burden. At her mother's deathbed, Mom promised her that her four sisters and brothers would never go into an orphanage. Instead, she took them in to live with us, followed by her father, then her father-in-law, until our house was full to the brim. She cared for them all, and they were with us until they left, either by death, or by marriage. But still our home was never empty. Our door was always open -- to friends and strangers alike ? Coffeepot always ready so she could sit down and help with their problems.

Whenever she felt an injustice was being done within our city, she approached City Council and worked until it was corrected. She had only completed sixth grade, staying home to nurse her mother due to her severe illness, but she frequently surprised the Council, and many others, with her brilliant knowledge.

And she worked miracles, many times. One of the biggest was when my sister's fiance called to say he was coming home in three weeks on military leave, and wanted to get married -- between Christmas and New Year's Eve! My mother went into action, and in three weeks my sister was wed -- in a full church ceremony, with 300 guests, a rented hall, catered food, and an orchestra for entertainment. She had done in three weeks what normally takes a year, all because she wanted her daughter to have a proper wedding, and it was perfect.

She taught us strength, caring for others, and a highly positive outlook on life. She was my Mother -- to me the most wonderful woman in the world.

—Kay Presto

Dedicated to Mary Blossey Vogel, and even for her little size, she was such a tower of strength...

Worthiness

Ask for what you want and be prepared to get it.
—Maya Angelou, American poet, writer, and actress

...to be loved, happy, not to settle for something less than you deserve.
—Jennifer Aniston, actress

No matter what age you are, or what your circumstances might be, you are special, and you still have something unique to offer.
Your life, because of who you are, has meaning.

Living with integrity means:
• Not settling for less than what you know you deserve
  in your relationships.
• Asking for what you want and need from others.
• Speaking your truth, even though it might create conflict or tension.
• Behaving in ways that are in harmony with your personal values.
• Making choices based on what you believe, and not what
  others believe.
—Barbara De Angelis, Speaker, Author

Inner self-worth and self-esteem are the most important things a woman can possess... When our self-worth is strong, we will not accept positions of inferiority and abuse.
—Louise L. Hay, Speaker, Author *Empowering Women*

A person's worth is contingent upon who he is, not upon what he does, or how much she has. The worth of a person, or a thing, or an idea, is in being, not in doing, not in having.
—Alice Mary Hilton

Love... when we love and accept ourselves, we shine.
To shine, we must be true to ourselves whether it be in our choice
of career, expressing our truth during a conflict, or taking care of
ourselves. Self-love is the foundation of any sparkle we hope to
create in this world. And when we love and accept ourselves, we
create sparkle for all to see.
—Annmarie Lardieri, www.RelationshipRenaissance.com

Your Being is an unfathomable mystery of wonder and beauty.
Turn your gaze inward and see what is there. Then, honor that Being.
—Peggy O'Neill, Speaker, Author *Walking Tall:Overcoming Inner
Smallness No Matter What Size You Are*, Small Miracles Unlimited,
www.YoPeggy.com

I am Woman - Hear me ROAR!
—Helen Reddy, Singer, Songwriter

Remember always that you have not only a right to be an individual,
you have an obligation to be one. You cannot make any useful
contribution in life unless you do this.
—Eleanor Roosevelt

The least of things with a meaning is worth more in life
than the greatest of things without it.
—Unknown

You don't get what you deserve.
You get what you THINK you deserve.
—Oprah Winfrey

Journaling Worksheets

What I Cherish About My Mother

In my earliest memories of my Mother, she was...

_____

_____

_____

As a teenager, I remember....
(a memory, an experience, a conversation...)

_____

_____

_____

_____

Holiday memories I remember...
(traditions, special gifts, family times, quality time)

_____

_____

_____

_____

_____

_____

The funniest thing(s) I remember about my Mother...

_____

_____

_____

_____

_____

What I most admire/respect about my mother is/was...

_____
_____
_____
_____
_____

How I am most like my Mother (looks, sayings, personality)

_____
_____
_____
_____

How I would like to be more like my Mother

_____
_____
_____
_____
_____

Our most memorable time(s) together...

_____
_____
_____
_____

My mother is special to me because...

_____
_____
_____
_____

My name was chosen because

_____
_____

What I Learned From My Mother

What I learned about LIFE from my Mother
(facing challenges, attitude, relationships...)

_____
_____
_____
_____
_____
_____
_____

What I learned about being a WOMAN/MAN from my Mother

_____
_____
_____
_____
_____

What I learned about being a MOTHER/FATHER

_____
_____
_____
_____
_____

What I learned about LOVE from my Mother

_____
_____
_____
_____
_____

Conversations I would love to have...

Mother, things I wish I had spoken to you about, include

_____

_____

_____

_____

_____

_____

_____

_____

_____

Mother, I never told you...

_____

_____

_____

_____

_____

_____

_____

_____

_____

_____

_____

_____

_____

_____

_____

_____

_____

Sheryl Roush

Sparkle-Tude™ Expert Sheryl Roush presents inspirational programs that rekindle the spirit, raise the bar, and create excitement.

Humorous, creative and authentic, she relates real-life experiences in a positive, lighthearted way that enriches the soul. She playfully engages audiences, offering valuable how-to tips while entertaining with stories, songs and surprises. Audiences "experience" her presentations - with lasting feelings, results, and significance.

Participants throughout Australia, Canada, England, Malaysia, Northern Ireland, Puerto Rico, Singapore, and the US have awarded her top-ratings for content, interaction and delivery style.

She was only the third woman in the world to earn the elite status of Accredited Speaker as honored by Toastmasters International (now in seventy countries) for outstanding platform professionalism. Sheryl was crowned "Ms. Heart of San Diego" for 2004 and 2005 for contributions to the community.

Sheryl has presented on programs alongside celebrities including: Olivia Newton-John, Jane Seymour, Art Linkletter, Thurl Bailey, *Good Morning America's* Joan Lunden, *Men are from Mars* John Gray, *Chicken Soup for the Soul's* Mark Victor Hansen, *One-minute Millionaire's* Robert G. Allen, and keynote closed for *Commander in Chief's* Geena Davis.

Have Sheryl present an energizing keynote opening—or wrap-up sensational closing—for your conference!

Highly-customized workshops, special events and retreat facilitation.

Sparkle Presentations
Sheryl@SparklePresentations.com
www. SparklePresentations.com
Call Toll Free (800) 932-0973 to schedule!

Are low morale, high-stress and poor attitudes affecting your customer service, productivity and teamwork today?

Need to rekindle the spirit on your organization?

Bring in the Sparkle-Tude™ Expert to energize positive trends!

Programs include:

Sparkle-Tude!™   Keeping a Sparkling Attitude Every Day
•Discover 7 Sparkle-Tude™ Boosters for home, work and life
•Learn how to deal with difficult people and challenging situations
•Enjoy 67 ways to stay sane and lighthearted in stressful times

Creating a Positive Work Environment
Tips and ideas to bring positive attitudes, connection and spirit to work. Morale-boosting team communication tactics and cooperation!

Customer Service with Heart
Enhanced interpersonal, communication and sales skills with attitude-boosters to generate authentic and exceptional service.

Humor in the Workplace
Discover tips to build morale, teamwork and cooperation, boost creativity, and lower mistakes while bringing lightheartedness into your organization.

Audiences include:

7-Up
AT&T
ChildStart
Ernst & Young
IBM
Intuit/Turbo Tax
Kiddie Academy
Loews Coronado Resorts
McMillin Realty
Mitsubishi
San Diego Zoo
Sheraton
Sony
UC-Berkeley
Union Bank
US Census Bureau
Verizon Wireless
Westin Hotels

Abbott Laboratories
Baptist Memorial Health Care Corp.
Bucknell University - Small Business Dev.
County of Los Angeles - Management
    and Secretarial Councils
    Sherrif's Department
    Dept. of Social Services
GlaxoSmithKline
Hong Kong Baptist University
Institute of Real Estate Management
Kaiser Permanente Physician Recruiters
Latham & Watkins, int'l law firm
Los Angeles Unified Schools (120 programs)
Phillips Morris of Asia, Hong Kong
Sharp Healthcare
Singapore Press
Stampin' Up! direct sales
Women's Council of Realtors

Index

Index

Order Form

[ ] AudioCD *Attitude: The Healthy Alternative* $19.95
    (Hilarious! Customized for women, presented after Olivia Newton-John)
[ ] CD-Rom *Attitude: The Healthy Alternative* $19.95
[ ] VHS Video *Attitude: The Healthy Alternative* $29.95
[ ] DVD *Attitude: The Healthy Alternative* $19.95
[ ] AudioCD *7 Ways to Connect with Your Audience* (for speakers/trainers)....$19.95
[ ] AudioCD *Sparkle-Tude: Women in Business* (live program)......................... $19.95
[ ] AudioCD *Sparkle When You Speak* (for women) speaking skills.................. $19.95
[ ] AudioCD *Solid Gold Marketing Tactics*.. $19.95
[ ] Book *Solid Gold Newsletter Design* (design brochures, fliers) $24.95
[ ] Book **Sparkle-Tudes!** Inspirational Quotes By and For Women $14.95
[ ] Book **Heart of a Woman** (poems, quotations, stories) $14.95
[ ] Book **Heart of a Mother** (poems, quotations, stories, tributes) $16.95
[ ] Book: *The Princess Principle: Women Helping Women Discover* $24.95
    Their Royal Spirit......18 stories of courage, hope, faith

        SUBTOTAL............................ $_____
        CA residents 7.75% sales tax.$_____
        12% Shipping & Handling..$_____
        ORDER TOTAL...................$_____

Name _____

Mailing Address _____

City_____State/Province_____

Country _____ Zip _____+_____

Telephone (_____) _____

Email : _____

[ ] Author Autograph– personalized inscription to read:
_____

Make checks payable to: Sparkle Presentations

Credit cards welcome
[ ] American Express   [ ] MasterCard   [ ] Visa   [ ] Discover

Card # _____

Expiration date _____ / _____ CID#(last 3-4 numbers on back of card)_____

Sparkle Presentations
P.O. Box 2373, La Mesa, CA 91943 USA
Sheryl@SparklePresentations.com
www. SparklePresentations.com
Phone orders: (858) 569-6555 or (800) 932-0973
Fax orders to: (858) 569-5924